AF439070

JUMP!

HOW TO BET ON YOURSELF, BUILD BOLDLY AND SCALE WITH PURPOSE

BLAKE SWAN

*To my family, my grounding and my joy—and to my father,
whose love and lessons continue to shape me.*

CONTENTS

NOTE TO READERS

This book was born out of the tension between success and fulfillment.

I wrote it for the entrepreneur who knows, deep down, they're meant for something bigger, not just more money or more accolades but more alignment, more clarity, and more freedom.

You don't need permission to jump. You just need to believe that what's on the other side is worth building for. I am here to guide you and allow you to learn from the lessons that I have learned on this incredible journey.

I hope this book gives you the permission you've been waiting for and the tools to trust yourself enough to leap.

To stay connected, explore bonus resources, or dive deeper into coaching opportunities, visit: *www.jumpwithblake.com*

■▶ INTRODUCTION

A sticky note.
That's what I got—after thirteen years of building someone else's dream.
No email. No meeting. No plan.
Just a yellow Post-it, curling at the edges, with three names scribbled in pen.

That was my "insight" into the division I'd poured my life into.
I stared at it like it might unfold into something bigger—something worthy.
It didn't.

Was this what I was worth?
After the midnight intake calls …
After dreaming up systems in the shower …
After fighting tooth and nail for every case—not just to win but to grow the damn machine …

I'd bled for that place.
And all I got was a scrap of paper and silence.

On paper, I was thriving. Titles, numbers, wins.
But in that moment, I felt hollow. Airless.
The office suddenly felt too small, like the air had been sucked out of it.

That was the day I crossed the False Finish Line—
where success looks impressive but feels like suffocation.

Where the mountain you just climbed turns out to be someone else's.

But that sticky note didn't mark the end.
It marked the beginning.

I tucked it into my desk drawer—not as a souvenir
but as a line in the sand.
A vow: I would never hand my life over that cheaply again.

Since then, I've built several businesses—some under my own name, others in partnership, including a law firm and a med spa—and together, we've scaled them far beyond what I thought was possible.
But more importantly, I built a life that finally feels like mine.

This book is for you if:

- You've checked all the boxes and still feel like something's missing.
- Living inside someone else's dream feels like you're slowly disappearing.
- You've reached your goals—but you know, deep down, they were never really yours.

If that's you, then you're in **the Fog**—
that disorienting space between the life you know and the one you can't yet name.

This book is your compass out of the Fog. It doesn't just help you escape—it helps you remember. Who you are. Why you're here. And how to build a life that doesn't require escape at all.
This is your guide to jump.

To jump out of the safety of the known and into the truth of what you're meant to build.
To stop climbing the wrong mountain and start building your own.
To trade in your False Finish Line for the real thing—
the one defined by purpose, ownership, and freedom.

I built a life that finally feels like mine. **I wrote this book so you can take your jump—with clarity, courage, and a hell of a lot more freedom.**

The Slow Death of the Dream

The sticky note didn't come out of nowhere. It was just the final straw.
For years, I held on to the belief that I would one day become a partner.
That belief kept me working late, generating massive revenue, and pushing past burnout.

There were conversations that hinted at ownership.
Promises floated but never landed.
Lunches filled with strategy talk somehow never led to clarity.

Each time I asked about financials, I was met with vague answers or brushed aside.
Then came the day I finally asked to be compensated like a partner.

The response:
"My partners have been trying cases since you were in diapers."

It didn't sting.
It clarified.

Get ready to JUMP.
Because when someone shows you where you stand, believe them.

He wasn't a villain.
He was a mirror—reflecting all the ways I'd delayed my own leap.
All the ways I clung to a story that said I needed permission to build something big.

I didn't lose hope all at once.
I lost it in pieces—
One unreturned email,
One vague promise,
One spreadsheet I was never shown.

In the end, he didn't need to change.
I did.

The sticky note wasn't disrespect.
It was a message:
No one is coming to give you the future you want. You have to claim it.

So, take a breath. And get ready to jump!

CHAPTER ONE

THE SIGNAL: HEARING THE CALL BEFORE THE JUMP

"The life you crave is pulling you for a reason."

THIS BOOK EXISTS BECAUSE I BELIEVE IN YOUR POTENTIAL. I believe in your ability to grow, to evolve, and to create a life that feels authentic and fulfilling. I know what it feels like to stand at the edge of change, overwhelmed by doubt and fear.

Maybe you've been there too. On paper, everything adds up—you hit your targets, keep things smooth, and follow the expected path. But inside, there's that quiet ache—the Signal. The knowing that you're meant for more.

For me, the Signal came as a spontaneous moment. I sat on my back patio after work, the air thick with humidity and silence. My chest felt like it was caving in—tight, hot, suffocating. I stood up so fast that the chair scraped across the wood. My hands clenched the railing. And then, I heard myself blurt out:

"Let's f*ing go!"

It was the first moment I let the truth move through my body before I could speak it. Something had to change.

I felt it in my body before I ever named it—a discontent, a lack of fulfillment, a pull. A knowing that something was missing and that I would have to change to find it.

Growing up in Connecticut as the youngest of four siblings, I was shaped by a competitive family dynamic that left me constantly trying to prove myself. My mom, one of seven children, came from a household where attention had to be earned, and that same intensity filtered into our home. My cousins were held up as examples of discipline and success, while I was often labeled as disorganized and forgetful.

I can still hear the comments—thinly veiled as jokes or casual observations—about how I would never keep up or how prep school would be the end of me. My grandfather, a brilliant Wharton graduate and stockbroker, had set a high bar for success, and in our family, falling short wasn't an option. College wasn't just encouraged—it was a requirement. The message was clear: if you didn't excel, you didn't belong.

As a child, I internalized these narratives. They taught me to retreat, to avoid confrontation, and to hide when I felt small. Survival meant invisibility. But as I got older, invisibility wasn't enough. By the time I was a teenager, I had grown tired of being underestimated. My frustration turned into defensiveness, and I developed a sharp tongue to shield myself from the pain of feeling inadequate.

Looking back, I see how much these patterns influenced my adult life. The same fight-or-flight tendencies that helped me navigate childhood carried into my career. I built walls, avoided vulnerability, and treated professional relationships with guarded friendliness. When I felt undervalued at work, I pulled away instead of leaning in.

These habits kept me in survival mode. I didn't yet understand that the hollowness I felt wasn't failure—it was the Signal. The quiet sign that I was winning the wrong game.

This was my False Finish Line: I had the title, the metrics, the recognition … but none of it silenced the ache.

I was one of the highest-producing associates in the firm. I hoped equity would quiet the ache. Instead, I was grinding for a title that was never coming.

But the longer I stayed, the clearer it became: I wasn't being groomed for ownership. I was being used to stabilize someone else's system. When I asked about financials or brought up growth, I was redirected—told to settle more cases instead. I didn't have access to the levers of leadership—I just helped turn the wheel.

And even that might have been enough—if everything else in my life hadn't fallen apart at once.

I found out we lost the pregnancy over the phone—I couldn't be there because of COVID. But I'll never forget the sound of my wife's voice. It wasn't just grief. It was fear. I raced to the doctor's office, heart pounding, praying I'd get there in time to hold her. She was waiting in the parking lot. When she saw me, she fell into my arms—and for a moment, time stopped. All the metrics, all the grind, all the future plans we thought we'd made—none of it mattered. Just her pain. Just our loss.

At the same time, my father's health spiraled. I spent nights pacing, praying, running—trying to keep both of them alive in different ways. Meanwhile, my compensation changed, and my responsibilities increased. I was more embedded in the system than ever—and yet more disconnected from my purpose.

All of it converged into a kind of quiet breaking point. The dream I'd been chasing began to fracture—not with a bang but with a series of subtle truths that became impossible to ignore.

You might be in the Signal phase right now. You haven't left. You haven't fully committed. But you know. Deep down, you already know.

I wasn't stuck. I was silent.

It wasn't a breakdown. It was a beginning.

This book is about that moment. The one where you stop waiting. The one where you hear the pull and decide to move toward it, even if you can't see where it ends.

Because that pull doesn't just change your mindset—it changes how you carry yourself, which leads you to your aligned opportunities. When you stop chasing validation and start building in alignment, your role shifts. You go from operator to architect, from reacting to leading.

This book will show you how to make that shift—step by step. It's built around a framework I call the JUMP Method: a four-part journey that begins with justifying your why, moves through uncovering limiting beliefs and shifting your mindset, and ends with planning your leap into something better.

You don't have to jump today. But you do have to listen to the Signal.

That's what this book is. Your signal. Your mirror. Your map.

Reflection Prompt: Your Signal

Recall a moment when you heard your Signal. Describe it, even if it didn't make sense at the time.

In the next chapter, we'll unpack why the Signal is often followed by silence—and how to move from confusion into clarity.

CHAPTER TWO

THE GRAVITY HOLDING YOU DOWN

"Comfort clips your wings before you ever leave the ground."

IF YOU DON'T MAKE THE JUMP, WHAT'S AT STAKE ISN'T JUST unrealized potential—it's the legacy you leave behind. For me, it's the fear of sitting in a casket one day with my children looking over and the energy of regret in the room. It's the possibility of not being the father, husband, and creator that gives purpose to my life.

Steven Pressfield, in *The War of Art*, warns that when we give in to resistance, we lose the chance to become who we were meant to be. Brené Brown, in *Daring Greatly*, reminds us that comfort may protect us from risk, but it slowly chips away at our growth and potential.

When my father was on his deathbed, he told me he didn't know what was next, but he just loved living so much. I can't imagine facing the end without that same feeling. I want to squeeze every last drop out of this journey—not out of fear, but because I deserve to. And I want that for you, too. A life so aligned and deeply yours that you'll look back on it with nothing but love.

The unknown scares people because it shines a light on their unlived potential. Bronnie Ware's *The Top Five Regrets of the Dying* reveals that many regret not living a life true to themselves. That regret terrifies me. I want a life where I show up fully. What would it mean for you to do the same—to live so boldly that regret has no room to grow?

I learned this lesson deeply during a retreat in New Mexico. The barn sat at the end of a dirt road on a mountainside.

Alone with my thoughts, I had no distractions. Then, Jana, the retreat leader, arrived.

In that serene environment, she confronted me with direct honesty. Her words landed like cold water to the face

Each morning began with twenty-five minutes of stillness. At first, it was excruciating. My foot bounced nervously, my head spun in circles, and I shifted on the couch like I was sitting on nails. But by the end, I had become the observer of my thoughts rather than the prisoner of them. I saw my fears and limiting beliefs for what they were—just stories.

Jana helped me reconnect with who I was before the world told me who to be. She challenged my beliefs, forced me to forgive, and guided me to take full responsibility for my life. That retreat became the turning point. It laid the foundation for the JUMP Method and the life I live now.

The stakes are high. This is about the fullness of your life, your impact, and the story you'll leave behind.

When I promised myself I'd leave the firm, I had no idea how. I needed a framework. I knew I had to plan, but I didn't anticipate the emotional weight—the vulnerability, fear, and uncertainty. I learned through doing, through mistakes that became lessons. My hope is that this book spares you some of that trial and shows you how to move forward—both practically and emotionally.

Most people don't stay because they're happy.
They stay because they've already paid too much to leave.

We like to believe we're logical beings, weighing pros and cons and making smart moves.

But the truth?

Most people don't jump—not because they're afraid of what's out there—but because they're too emotionally invested in where they are.

They've already sunk years into a path that no longer feels right. They've built reputations, routines, relationships. Leaving would feel like betrayal—not just of others but of the version of themselves who worked so hard to get here.

It's not fear of failure that traps us.

It's the **sunk cost of identity**.

The Emotional Mortgage

Imagine your life like a house.

You bought it young. Painted the walls. Put up photos. You even got used to the creaky floorboards and weird plumbing. Over time, you convinced yourself it's your house—even if it never really felt like home.

Now, you're staring at a new one. Bigger, brighter, maybe closer to who you really are. But to move in, you'd have to walk away from all those "payments" you've made—the years, the identity, the approval, the predictability.

And so, you stay.

You keep paying the **emotional mortgage** on a house you no longer want to live in.

That's what most people do.

They stay in lives they've outgrown—because leaving would mean admitting the past wasn't the destination.
Just the road.

I know—because I paid that mortgage for years … on someone else's dream.

The Real Reason You're Stuck

If you're waiting for clarity before you jump, you'll wait forever. The fog doesn't clear from the shore—it lifts when you start walking.

The leap isn't logical.
It's emotional.

You don't need more data.
You need more **truth**.

And the truth is, the longer you wait, the heavier it gets. The job. The approval. The guilt. The mask.
Eventually, the dream **suffocates**—buried under the weight of everything you were afraid to lose.

Not because you weren't capable.

But because you didn't jump.

The JUMP Method: Your Path to Transformation

This framework didn't fall from the sky—it was forged in long nights, raw fears, and the quiet hell of second-guessing everything. I created the JUMP Method because I needed it. Maybe you do too.

The JUMP Method breaks the transformation into four essential steps. Each one is designed to help you see clearly, move honestly, and build intentionally. It's not just about breaking free. It's about building what comes next.

What follows is just a glimpse—each step will unfold more deeply in the coming chapters. But for now, here's the blueprint that changed my life.

J: Justify Your Why

Before you leap, identify the reason behind your desire for change. Why do you need to jump? What's at stake if you don't?

Your "why" is your foundation. It will carry you through doubt and resistance. Viktor Frankl wrote: "Those who have a 'why' to live can bear with almost any 'how.'" Simon Sinek echoes this: "People don't buy what you do—they buy why you do it."

For me, regret was the greatest threat. I didn't want to just exist. I wanted to live a life of purpose and meaning. What's your "why"?

U: Uncover Limiting Beliefs

Next, identify the beliefs that hold you back. These often come from past experiences or societal expectations. They're invisible chains keeping you stuck.

Henry Ford said, "Whether you think you can, or you think you can't—you're right." Tony Robbins adds, "The only thing that's keeping you from getting what you want is the story you keep telling yourself."

Be honest. Challenge what you've been taught to believe. Ask if your fears are facts—or just familiar.

M: Mindset Shift

Transformation begins with mindset. Without it, fear will keep you stuck.

Carol Dweck wrote, "Becoming is better than being." Wayne Dyer added, "If you change the way you look at things, the things you look at change."

A shift in perspective is power. It helps you embrace growth, see opportunity, and rewire your brain to act from courage instead of fear.

P: Plan and Take Small Leaps

You don't have to jump all at once. Break your leap into small, manageable steps.

Lao Tzu reminds us, "The journey of a thousand miles begins with one step." James Clear, in *Atomic Habits*, wrote, "You do not rise to the level of your goals. You fall to the level of your systems."

Start small. Build momentum. Test and adjust. It's about consistency, not perfection.

Now, take a moment to reflect: What's your "why"? What are your goals for your jump? What would success look like?

Define them. Then set a date. That's the first real step.

You've already started your transformation by reading this far. Now it's time to commit.

Reflection Prompt: Your Emotional Mortgage

- Where are you still paying an emotional mortgage?
- What identity are you clinging to that no longer serves the version of you who's waking up?

Mini Action Step

Write a letter to the version of yourself who stayed too long. Tell them what you see now.

Then, write a one-line declaration of what you're stepping into next.

In the next chapter, we'll surface the hidden beliefs quietly keeping you stuck—and teach you how to cut the anchor before it becomes your identity.

CHAPTER THREE

YOU WERE ALWAYS MEANT TO FLY

"Your soul remembers what your fear forgot: you were built to soar."

The Comfort of Familiarity

Many people feel stuck in their jobs, even when they appear "successful" on paper. They cling to the comfort of familiarity—much like in *Who Moved My Cheese?*, where the characters hesitate to leave the known for new opportunities. A steady paycheck and predictable routine create a false sense of security, quietly trapping ambitious people in lives that no longer align with their passions or instincts.

Familiarity feels safe. It offers stability, routine, and predictability. But over time, it numbs ambition. For many high performers, this becomes **the cage of familiarity**—comfortable enough to stay yet confining enough to suppress your potential.

You don't recognize it as a cage until you try to grow. What once felt like structure becomes stagnation. You think you're being responsible, but you didn't build a life; you built a boundary. And now, it's time to break it.

That's the moment of truth.
The moment you realize this isn't just about your job—it's about your identity.

Breaking the frame means acknowledging that the structure you once built for safety—your title, your routines, your reputation—may now be limiting your evolution. It's the uncomfortable moment when your dreams begin to outgrow your environment. Growth demands you stop reinforcing what no longer fits and start designing what actually reflects who you're becoming.

So, ask yourself: Are you sticking to routines simply because they're familiar—even if they no longer challenge or excite you? Are you choosing predictability over possibility? The illusion of safety is often the most dangerous trap for entrepreneurial minds. True growth begins not when you feel ready but when you're willing to step beyond what once felt safe.

This instinct to hold on to the familiar isn't just psychological—it's biological.
Familiarity isn't just a preference; it's a survival mechanism.

Your brain is wired to protect you, not to evolve you. It craves predictability because predictability once meant staying alive. For our ancestors, stepping into the unknown could have meant getting eaten, exiled, or injured. That wiring still exists, even though the threats have changed. Today, unfamiliar territory doesn't mean predators; it means possibility. And yet, your nervous system still interprets change as danger.

That's why leaving a job—even one that drains you—can feel like walking off a cliff. When you think about walking away from what's known, your brain starts sounding the alarm: *What if I fail? What if I lose everything? What if I'm not enough?* These aren't just thoughts; they're protective patterns.

And they show up strongest right when you're on the edge of change.

I had multiple bar licenses, a solid reputation, and a growing skill set. But I was still terrified to leave my job. I was the sole provider for my family. I was afraid of making a mistake I couldn't come back from. Looking back, I realize now that I wasn't afraid of failure. I was afraid of uncertainty.

This is what makes the jump so difficult. Not the lack of skill. Not the logistics.
The fear.

Because your brain will always try to trade long-term fulfillment for short-term safety. It doesn't care about your potential; it cares about your protection.

These risks, though not life-threatening in the traditional sense, are why it's crucial to take calculated risks and plan carefully, as I'll walk you through later in this book.

But here's the shift:
When you understand that your fear is biological, not personal, you can stop letting it drive the car. You can acknowledge it, thank it for trying to protect you, and then move forward anyway. Growth isn't about eliminating fear. It's about developing a new relationship with it.

Familiarity and the Lens It Creates

Familiarity doesn't just impact your actions—it reshapes your perception. The longer you stay inside predictable systems and routines, the more those systems start to feel like truth.

You don't just get used to the way things are; you begin to believe that's the way they have to be.

This is the lens of familiarity. It's subtle but powerful.
It whispers questions like:

- "Is this really just how the industry works?"
- "Is this the only way to succeed—or just the only way I've seen?"
- "Do people like me really have to follow this path—or have I just never seen another option?"

And these questions rarely get asked because familiarity convinces you that what you've always seen is all that exists.

Early in my entrepreneurial journey, I didn't realize how much of my thinking was still shaped by the firm I had left. I assumed I was starting fresh, but in reality, I was still looking through a lens shaped by familiarity. It wasn't until I met my law partner that I started to challenge that lens. He brought different experiences, different strategies, and a different vision. And for the first time, I asked myself, *Are the structures I'm clinging to actually helping me—or just comfortable?* That question changed everything.

Now, I surround myself with people who challenge what I think is "normal." I'm in Masterminds. I have a business coach. I actively seek out friction—not because I like being wrong but because I've learned that tension is a gateway to clarity. I am constantly asking myself if there is a better way.

Because here's the truth:
When you live too long inside the lens of familiarity, you risk mistaking your frame of reference for reality.

When you challenge the lens of familiarity, everything shifts.

You stop seeing the world as fixed and start seeing it as flexible. You begin to question the norms you inherited, the systems you followed, and the structures that once made you feel safe. And when that happens, something powerful emerges: possibility.

The truth is, most of what you were taught was about survival, not innovation. It was designed to get you in the door, not to show you how to build your own. That's why entrepreneurship demands something deeper: the ability to question what you were handed and rebuild what actually works for who you are becoming.

Real innovation doesn't begin with ideas; it begins with disobedience.
It starts when you ask, *What if there's a better way?*

That question saved my business.

Early on, I caught myself repeating the exact systems I had learned at my old firm. Not because they were effective but because they were familiar. I had left the job, but I was still living by its rules. Familiarity had crept into my foundation. And like a virus in the code, it was quietly corrupting what I was trying to build.

It wasn't until I partnered with someone who thought completely differently that I began to see what was possible. He hadn't been trained the same way I had. He hadn't internalized the same limitations. He asked questions I never thought to ask. He broke the model I had unconsciously been clinging to.

And I realized: the greatest threat to innovation is unexamined repetition.

The same patterns that limit individuals also take down giants. They keep solving yesterday's problems with yesterday's thinking. And eventually, they get passed by.

Let me show you what that looks like:

- **Kodak** invented the digital camera but refused to embrace it, fearing it would cannibalize their film business. That fear cost them everything.
- **Blockbuster** had a chance to buy Netflix for fifty million dollars and turned it down. They couldn't imagine a world without physical rentals. Netflix could.
- **Nokia** once led the mobile phone industry but failed to adapt when smartphones emerged. Their comfort with the status quo became their downfall.

Each of these companies died at the altar of familiarity.

But the ones that thrive? They break their own models before the world does.

- **Netflix** didn't wait to be disrupted—they disrupted themselves. They moved from DVDs to streaming and from streaming to creating.
- **Apple** didn't just innovate once. They kept pushing—replacing their own products, reinventing their ecosystem, and expanding into entirely new markets. Their growth didn't come from clinging to what worked; it came from outgrowing it.

These aren't just business case studies. They're cautionary tales for anyone building something new.

Because the truth is:
What once made you great will eventually hold you back—if you don't evolve.

Familiarity can *feel* like success. A steady paycheck, a structured calendar, a business that runs smoothly … It's easy to mistake predictability for progress. But if you're not careful, that comfort becomes the ceiling. And growth doesn't live under ceilings.

Good Leaders Embrace the Unfamiliar

The best business leaders are comfortable with the unfamiliar. They invite new ideas, challenge the status quo, and foster an environment where innovation thrives. Stepping outside the familiar ensures their businesses stay relevant, innovative, and growing.

Fixed Versus Growth Mindset

This shift from familiarity to fulfillment often requires a mindset shift. Drawing on Carol Dweck's book *Mindset*, those with a fixed mindset believe their abilities are limited, which discourages them from pursuing entrepreneurship. They believe they are only capable of doing what they already know, so they stay in familiar environments that reinforce their comfort zone.

This mindset shift is essential when deciding to leave a nine-to-five job. A fixed mindset will keep you tethered to the comfort of familiarity, but a growth mindset will empower you to see these challenges of entrepreneurship as stepping-stones to achieving your full potential.

I always dreamed bigger than my environment. From the very first month I joined the firm, while their vision was for me to handle depositions, I wanted to push beyond that. When I took over the Tennessee operation, my vision wasn't just to manage cases—I wanted to scale the operation, expand it, and make it as profitable as possible.

A defining moment came during my last lunch with my boss. He observed that it seemed like I was trying to take over the world, while he was content with the life and business he had built. It was a sincere, honest conversation, and I realized he was in wealth-preservation mode, while I was in wealth-building mode. That moment confirmed what I already knew: my dreams were bigger than the box I was in.

Now, the day I left the firm wasn't just a career move; it was an explosion of the box I had been confined to. The familiarity of that role had become too limiting for my vision. Since then, I have built something that I am proud of, that people want to be a part of, and that some even want to buy. But the vision of any buyer would have to be quite large because right now, there are no limits. My firm grows every day, and I have the freedom to shape it according to my own vision. I no longer operate within someone else's system—I'm building my own. I want that for you, which is why I am sharing my JUMP Method so that you, too, can have the freedom to create the business you want.

Entrepreneurship has allowed me to wake up every day with curiosity, excitement, and the freedom to create. Nothing will fill your heart like waking up every day with the ability and freedom to build your dream. The freedom I've embraced is something I wouldn't trade for the comfort of familiarity, no matter how secure it once seemed.

My life now is all about building and creating. Every day is different and full of opportunity. I'm constantly thinking about what new systems we can implement, how we can improve recruitment to get the best staff and paralegals, and which marketing methods we need to employ. I'm tracking our numbers, responding to both positive and negative data, and figuring out how to adjust and improve. I think about how to motivate my team and how we can provide the best possible client experience. I'm not just a part of the machine anymore—I'm building the machine.

I've learned that the vision has to be big enough to fit everyone else's vision within it. My vision for growth expands daily, and it now includes my team and their own dreams. I recently attended a conference where the speaker asked everyone about their goals. After reflecting, I realized that many people's goals in that room could have fit within mine.

As I've leaned into the unfamiliar, I've started to attract like-minded individuals with the same mindset. That's why I now co-own a med spa with a well-known doctor who is expanding her brand across the country. My law partner is one of the most inspirational and driven people I've ever met. His vision is aligned with mine, but his mindset pushes me to allow my vision to evolve and grow.

Now, don't get me wrong. The challenges of entrepreneurship are real. There are no guarantees, and many people overlook the risks—financial, emotional, and strategic. Entrepreneurs face unexpected obstacles, uncertainty, and times when things don't go as planned. But those who succeed are the ones who adapt, pivot, and continuously learn while focusing on what they can control.

Because here's the truth: **the sky didn't move—they just stopped pretending their cage was a ceiling.**

When you blow the doors off your old limitations, you invite powerful collaborators into your life—people who want to build and create alongside you. As a coach, I guide entrepreneurs to build their dreams by providing practical steps and helping them uncover what's holding them back. Through this process, many of them find that leaders in their industry don't just take notice but actively want to collaborate. They also begin to realize that the rooms they're in are of a completely different caliber than ever before. And when you upgrade the room you're in, you upgrade your network, yourself, and your business.

We'll explore how to take your next leap in the following chapter.

CHAPTER FOUR

WHAT IT REALLY MEANS TO BE AN ENTREPRENEUR

ENTREPRENEURSHIP IS OFTEN ROMANTICIZED AS FREEDOM and flexibility, but the reality in the beginning comes with more responsibility and effort than a traditional nine-to-five job. It's about more than just doing what you love or controlling your schedule—it's about building something that's yours. In the beginning, you'll wear many hats—handling everything from managing cash flow to recruiting your team and making tough decisions without the safety net of a boss or a predictable salary.

You're signing up for the reality that the success you crave won't come overnight. It will require patience, grit, and a high tolerance for risk and uncertainty. Entrepreneurship demands endurance—because while the rewards can be great, they are often hard-earned.

Success for an entrepreneur is building something in your image—crafting a vision that reflects your values, passions, and goals. It's about focusing on what drives you while delegating tasks to individuals who not only excel at what they do but genuinely enjoy the things you don't. True success lies in assembling a team that complements your strengths, freeing you to spend your time on what truly matters.

When I first stepped into entrepreneurship, I believed I had to do it all. It wasn't until I brought in a trusted partner to to focus on the parts of the business that I did not enjoy, that I found the freedom to focus on scaling, strategy, and the creative aspects I loved. I didn't realize it then, but my high performance had become my armor—a defense mechanism I mistook for strength, and one I'd later learn to recognize and unpack. Delegating didn't just lighten my load; it made the business stronger.

I had opened an office in Tennessee but still lived in Florida, so if a client wanted to meet in person, I would fly up on the spot. I wouldn't hesitate or negotiate. I'd just ask, "When?" and make it happen. That's what it meant to build something from scratch. Whatever it took, I did it.

In fact, I once missed out on a massive case because I was flying to North Carolina to visit my mother. I didn't have service for just two hours, and that short window of silence cost me the opportunity. I was still small then. Every connection mattered. Every lead was vital. And that loss? It stung. It was a vivid reminder that building something of your own means being on—always.

Success, for me, was realizing that I didn't have to do everything myself and that collaboration could bring my vision to life in ways I hadn't imagined.

Entrepreneurship isn't just about creating financial wealth; it's about building a life and a business that reflect your values. It's the freedom to choose how you spend your time, the joy of seeing your ideas take shape, and the fulfillment of knowing you've built something meaningful—not just for yourself but for those around you. Entrepreneurship can take many forms—starting something from scratch, scaling a team, or bringing entrepreneurial thinking into a larger organization. What matters isn't the structure but that you're building in alignment with your values and vision.

If you're driven by the desire to create, build, and own your future, entrepreneurship offers a sense of fulfillment that most nine-to-five jobs cannot. It provides the freedom to innovate, fail, and improve. For those with an entrepreneurial spirit burning inside, no amount of comfort or security in a traditional job will ever satisfy. Unless that entrepreneurial spirit is allowed to flourish, the choice isn't just between a nine-to-five and entrepreneurship—it's between fulfillment or a lack thereof.

These are concepts we will explore further in the next chapter. As you continue through this book, you'll learn to break free from familiarity in a strategic and sustainable way. The JUMP Method will help you build that bridge, and soon, you'll be taking steps toward your entrepreneurial vision, one small leap at a time.

By the end of this chapter, you should begin asking yourself some important questions:

- Are you truly fulfilled in your current role, or are you stuck in a cycle of comfort and familiarity?
- It's easy to remain in a job that provides security, routine, and predictability, but does that align with your deepest passions and goals?

That's the Gravity of Familiarity at work—the emotional force that pulls you back into what's known, even when it no longer fits. It feels safe, but it keeps you stuck. You don't cling to it because it's right—you cling because it's comfortable.

Familiarity may feel safe, but true fulfillment comes from stepping into the unknown and embracing growth. If you identify where you're clinging to routine, understand the societal and psychological forces at play, and begin to shift your mindset, you can start your journey toward a more entrepreneurial and fulfilling life.

Take a moment to reflect on your current life and career. Grab a journal and write down:

1. Where are you clinging to familiarity? What routines or habits provide comfort but no longer serve your bigger goals?

2. Imagine your life after the jump. What could it look like if you embraced change and moved toward your true purpose? Write out your vision for a more fulfilling, entrepreneurial life. What excites you? What scares you?

3. Identify one small step you can take today. Inspired by *Atomic Habits*, what small action can you take to move out of familiarity? This could be reading an article on entrepreneurship, brainstorming ideas, or reaching out to a mentor for advice.

4. Make a commitment. Once you've identified a small step, make a commitment to act on it within the next twenty-four hours. Small, consistent actions lead to transformation.

Take a moment to review your answers. You'll begin to see where familiarity is holding you back and start to make the shift toward a more fulfilling, entrepreneurial future.

In the coming chapters, we'll dive deeper into the JUMP Method, guiding you through the process of not only leaving your nine-to-five but also thriving as you build a life that aligns with your deepest values and desires. Your journey starts with recognizing that fulfillment lies beyond the comfort.

CHAPTER FIVE

CLEARING THE GROUND BEFORE TAKEOFF

"You can't take off carrying the weight of old stories."

You Were Meant for Something More

Entrepreneurs often feel trapped by structure, haunted, or perhaps blessed, by a deeper calling. This calling is purpose. It doesn't shout, but it pulls. It nudges you toward a life that feels bigger, more aligned, more yours.

You were meant to build. To lead. To live fully.

And if you don't jump, the calling won't go away. It will haunt you—through restlessness, dissatisfaction, and the aching sense that you're meant for more.

These feelings are not flaws. They're invitations. This chapter is about recognizing those inner signals as sacred clues, then aligning your strengths, your story, and your sense of self with the life that's calling to you.

Because the choice isn't just about staying stuck or stepping forward.

It's about deciding: Will you embrace your calling—or let it haunt you?

The Illusion of the Finish Line

For years, I chased validation, especially from my family. I pushed myself relentlessly, believing that if I just achieved enough, I'd finally feel fulfilled. I believed purpose lived at the end of some external milestone.

I remember driving home after acing a law school exam. I should've felt proud. Instead, I felt numb. I crashed into days of depression.

This wasn't a one-time thing. It was a pattern. After passing three bar exams—two while working full time—I still felt hollow. I kept telling myself the next achievement would be the one. But each time, I crossed the finish line … and nothing changed.

In my late thirties, I was overweight, drinking heavily almost every night, and still dragging myself to the gym at dawn. I saw a guy run a five-minute mile. I decided I had to do it, too. I trained. I pushed. I did it.

And I felt absolutely nothing.

Not relief. Not pride. Just more evidence that I was running from something—not toward it.

High performers often armor themselves with achievement. It looks like drive, but it's often self-doubt in disguise. Achievement became my armor—and my cage.

No finish line could give me what I really needed: permission to believe I mattered.

I didn't realize it then, but I was in pain. I just didn't know how to name it yet.

It wasn't until I confronted the internal lie I'd been carrying—that I wasn't enough—and began discovering my true purpose that I started living a life that felt like mine.

Deserving Because You Exist

One of the most life-changing truths I've ever learned is this:

You deserve to live fully and pursue your purpose simply because you exist.

But for years, I believed the opposite. I thought I had to

earn my worth—through performance, achievements, and constantly proving myself. I internalized a subtle but persistent story: that value had to be created, not claimed.

I was the youngest of four. My parents were deep into their careers by the time I came along. When my mom found out she was pregnant with me, she sent my dad a **sympathy wreath**. An actual funeral wreath. It became a running family joke—one we laughed about for years. I laughed too.

But that story stayed with me. I never thought I was a mistake. But I was unexpected. And when you grow up in a big, busy household, it's easy to feel like you have to **earn your place**. Like the way to matter is to be impressive.

So, I became impressive.

I chased good grades. I hit every milestone. I pushed harder than anyone else—not because I loved the pressure but because I thought it made me undeniable. That invisible drive followed me everywhere. If I could perform well enough, maybe I'd be seen. Maybe I'd be enough.

That's the thing about limiting beliefs—they often wear the mask of ambition.

But underneath the hustle is usually a question we haven't answered.

For me, it was:

"Do I matter enough to be seen without the achievement?"

It took me decades to realize that I didn't need to earn my worth. I needed to reclaim it.

That sympathy wreath used to feel like a punchline.

Now it feels like a metaphor.

Even before I arrived, I disrupted the plan.

And maybe … that was the plan.

The Already Worthy Principle

For years, I believed I had to do something remarkable to be worthy of love, success, or even rest. I'd accomplish something incredible—pass bar exams, close massive cases, outrun everyone in sight—and still feel like no one saw me.

But the truth is, you don't need applause to be enough.

You don't need to be perfect to be powerful.

I call this the Already Worthy Principle:

You don't prove your worth—you protect it.

You were born with it. The world may have tried to convince you otherwise. But the truth is already in you. Your job now is to stop handing that power away—to guard it, act from it, and build from it.

This shift in perspective is foundational to the JUMP Method. Because once you stop chasing external validation, you can start uncovering your limiting beliefs and embrace the unique purpose that's been inside you all along.

Breaking Free from the Comparison Trap

Even when we stop seeking approval, comparison still sneaks in the back door.

No matter how successful you are, there will always be someone who seems to be doing better—making more money, signing more clients, building a bigger brand. And in the age of social media, we're bombarded with highlight reels that make it easy to forget what's real.

But what you see on the surface is rarely the full truth.

That perfectly polished brand? Might be masking burnout.

That confident public speaker? Might go home and collapse in self-doubt.

As Charlie Munger once said:

"Envy is the dumbest of the seven deadly sins because it's the only one you can't have any fun at."

Envy offers nothing in return. It drains your energy and distracts you from your zone of impact.

The way out of comparison isn't willpower. It's alignment. Specifically, alignment with your **Zone of Genius**.

Discovering Your Zone of Genius

In his book *The Big Leap*, Gay Hendricks introduces the concept of the Zone of Genius—the space where your natural talents, passions, and purpose intersect.

It's the zone where your work feels effortless, fulfilling, and impactful. But getting there requires a shift because most of us spend our lives stuck in our **Zone of Excellence**: a place we're good at but not lit up by.

That was me at my nine-to-five. I was great at settling cases. I was an aggressive negotiator with a background in competitive sailboat racing, which gave me the edge to map leverage points and outmaneuver resistance. I was the person others came to when things got stuck.

But I was still stuck.

My real genius wasn't in closing cases. It was in building, creating, and inspiring others. It took years—and burnout—to realize it.

What I wasn't great at? Organization and small details. Those tasks drained me. But when I hired my first assistant— someone whose genius is in organizing chaos—I started to breathe. I started to scale. I started to **feel alive**.

That's the power of aligning with your genius. It's not just about *what* you do; it's about building the support around you that lets you stay there.

And that's the JUMP Method in motion:

- I *Justified* **My Why** by reconnecting to what I love.
- I *Uncovered* **Limiting Beliefs** that told me I had to do it all alone.

- I **Shifted My *Mindset*** around delegation and worth.
- I ***Planned* and Took Leaps** by building a team around my genius.

Exercise: Reflect on Your Zone of Genius

Use this to uncover patterns that point toward your unique purpose.

1. Look Back at Your Life:

- What tasks came naturally to you?
- When did you feel immersed, engaged, or "in flow"?

2. Write About Peak Moments:

- Identify three times you felt most alive.
- What were you doing? What skills were you using? How did it feel?

3. Look for Patterns:

- What themes keep coming up?

The answers that arise are your breadcrumbs. Follow them.

Your Genius Is Your Ikigai

Your **Zone of Genius** is the space where you feel most alive—where your natural talents and passions collide, and work feels like play. But genius alone isn't always enough to build a life or business. That's where *ikigai* comes in.

The Japanese concept of ikigai adds two more essential dimensions:

- **What the world needs** (impact)
- **What you can be paid for** (sustainability)

So, while your Zone of Genius is about *flow*, your ikigai is about *direction*—how you use that genius to serve others and sustain yourself.

What's the Difference?

Let's say your Zone of Genius is *storytelling*. You're naturally gifted at shaping ideas, drawing people in, and making meaning from chaos.

But that alone isn't ikigai.

Now imagine you take that storytelling ability and use it to:

Help business owners craft their brand narrative (**impact**)

Build a coaching practice or write a book (**sustainability**)

Do work you love and feel proud of (**passion + talent**)

That's ikigai—your genius applied intentionally, in service of both others and yourself.

Zone of Genius is your *internal power source.*

Ikigai is your *external compass.*

Now, consider what answers the following questions in this chart to gain more clarity on what these concepts point to for you.

Concept	Focus	Question It Answers
Zone of Genius	*Flow and Fulfillment*	"What makes me feel most alive?"
Ikigai	*Alignment and Impact*	"How can I use that to serve and sustain my life?"

Your Zone of Genius aligns with the Japanese concept of ikigai—the intersection of what you love, what you're good at, what the world needs, and what you can be paid for.

Ikigai = Purpose. And purpose fuels the jump.

Here's how it breaks down:

Ikigai Element	Reflection
What You Love (Passion)	What excites you? What would you do even if no one paid you?
What You're Good At (Talent)	What do people consistently praise you for?
What the World Needs (Impact)	How do your strengths solve real problems for others?
What You Can Be Paid For (Sustainability)	How can this create a livelihood?

When you find the overlap, your work stops feeling like work. It becomes a blueprint for a life that's not just profitable but **purposeful**.

Initiation Through Struggle: My Friend and My Father

I'll never forget the day my childhood best friend pulled into my driveway. At first, I was excited to see him. But as soon as he stepped out of his car, I saw it—the addiction carved into his face.

What I didn't realize at the time was that the pain I saw in him … was the same pain buried inside me. Unprocessed. Unheard. Ignored.

I took drastic action: I made him move in with me. Every morning at 5 a.m., I dragged him to work out, meditate, get clean. I thought I was mentoring him. Saving him. Leading him out of the darkness.

The practices I was enforcing on him were the exact ones I needed most.

Eventually, he broke. He finally admitted the truth, checked into rehab, and began to heal. And watching his bravery forced me to face my own addictions—my own emotional avoidance, my unhealthy reliance on alcohol, my refusal to slow down and feel.

At the same time, something else was breaking open in me: my father was dying.

Facing Death and Finding Peace

My dad had been on a ventilator more times than I can count. The first time shook me to my core. Time blurred. I remember walking miles just to keep from falling apart. I kept whispering to myself that I couldn't survive without him.

He was terrified of dying, and he admitted it. Not because he feared what came next but because he loved life so deeply. He didn't want to leave it.

Then came a breathwork journey that changed everything.

In that session, I became him. I was lying on a hospital bed, intubated. Each breath was a battle I couldn't win. The room seemed to fold in on itself, the walls pressing closer, the air thinning. Panic made my chest tighten and my breath even shallower. My body ached, fear surged through me, and I felt everything he had felt. Helpless. Terrified. And then—I died. But I didn't disappear.

I expanded.

On the other side of that moment was something I didn't expect: peace.

For the first time, I understood something my mind had never let me accept:

He could die … and I would still be okay.

He could be at peace. And so could I.

The Casket Dream

Shortly after that breathwork journey, I had a dream.

I was lying in a casket. My children stood over me—not crying, not panicking. Just … present. I felt no fear. Only pride.

I had lived well. I had loved well. And I felt free.

But even in the dream, I knew that outcome wasn't guaranteed. That kind of peace would require **different choices—now.**

And I'm grateful for that.

Because it reminded me: death isn't the enemy.

A life unlived is.

Reflection Exercise: Put Yourself in a Casket

This may sound morbid, but reflecting on death isn't about fear. It's about clarity.

In many cultures, contemplating mortality is a sacred tool for insight. It strips away the noise and surfaces what truly matters.

Close your eyes. Visualize your funeral.

Your loved ones are gathered around you. What do you want them to say?

Now ask yourself:

- What would need to change for that to become true?
- What fears, distractions, or patterns are pulling you out of alignment?
- What would you need to start doing *today* to feel proud at the end?

Your legacy is being written every day. Make sure you're the one holding the pen.

What My Father's Regrets Taught Me

Before my father passed, we had some of the most honest conversations of our lives.

He told me about his biggest regrets:

Not spending more time with family.

Not opening another funeral home after his brother pushed him into selling.

Not staying true to the work that gave his life purpose.

He had been a firefighter. A police officer. A mortician. His whole life had been about helping people through dark, painful moments. That work fulfilled him. When he walked away from it, something went quiet inside him.

He became a mirror for me.

I was working in a career that only fulfilled *part* of my purpose. I wasn't spending enough time with my family. I was doing what looked right on paper but not what felt aligned in my soul.

That conversation marked a shift. I realized:

If I didn't change, I would inherit the same regrets.

Purpose Versus Your Why

There's a difference between purpose and **your** why, and understanding this difference is crucial before taking your leap.

- Purpose is the path, the long arc of your life's meaning.
- Your why is the engine, the emotional driver that keeps you walking when the road gets steep.

Your why is almost always personal. It comes from your pain, your past, or your unmet needs.

Purpose gives you direction.

Your why gives you fuel.

My purpose is to build, to inspire, to teach.

But my why?

It's rooted in years of not believing any of that was possible for me.

When you uncover your why, the leap doesn't feel reckless. It feels inevitable.

Bringing It All Together

To clear the ground before takeoff, you must be willing to shed more than dead weight. You have to release the stories, beliefs, comparisons, and expectations that were never yours to carry in the first place.

That means:

- **Letting go of the lie** that you have to earn your worth.
- **Breaking free from the trap** of comparing your life to someone else's highlight reel.
- **Identifying your Zone of Genius**, not just for productivity—but for fulfillment.
- **Reflecting on your mortality**, not to dwell in fear—but to wake up.
- **Remembering your purpose** and preparing to unearth your why.

It's your runway.

This is the moment in the JUMP Method where the fog begins to clear.

Because when you know your purpose and you begin to understand your why,

You stop reacting.

You start creating.

You stop chasing worth.

You start building from it.

That's how you prepare to leap—not with reckless urgency but with grounded clarity.

Your JUMP in Motion

Let's look again at how the four pillars begin aligning right here:

Pillar	In Action
Justify Your Why	You're beginning to uncover the real reason you're being pulled toward something more.
Uncover Limiting Beliefs	You've identified stories about worth, comparison, fear, and identity that no longer serve you.
Mindset Shift	You've started releasing external validation and embracing internal truth.
Plan and Take Leaps	You've begun identifying your Zone of Genius and where you're meant to operate and scale.

This is the foundation.

And that's why this chapter is called "Clearing the Ground Before Takeoff."

Next Steps: The Power of Finding Your Why

In the next chapter, we'll go even deeper.

You'll explore the emotional root of your *why*—not just what you do or want to build but why it matters so deeply to you.

We'll uncover how your past—especially the parts you've tried to bury—holds the exact wisdom needed to shape your future.

Because once you understand your why, your decisions get sharper, your energy becomes focused, and your actions carry conviction.

No more drifting.

Just direction.

Real direction.

Reflection Prompt: Legacy, Genius, and Alignment

Grab your journal or a quiet space and take this moment seriously. This isn't just a chapter reflection. This is about your life.

1. Casket Clarity

Close your eyes. Picture your own funeral.

- What would you *want* to be remembered for?
- What do you *fear* being remembered for?
- What would have to change for the right story to be told?

2. Genius Inventory

Think of three moments where you felt deeply alive—what were you doing, and why did it feel effortless or meaningful?

3. Alignment Check

On a scale of one to ten, how aligned do you feel today with:

- Your purpose
- Your genius
- Your joy
- Your time

Now ask:

"What's one small but brave step I can take *this week* to realign?"

Mini Action Step: The Worth Reframe

Write this on a sticky note, in your Notes app, or wherever you'll see it daily:

"I don't prove my worth. I protect it."

Let that truth guide your decisions, your boundaries, your energy, and your leap.

Now It's Time to Justify Your Why

In the next chapter, we begin the core of the JUMP Method—**Justify Your Why**.

You'll go deeper into the difference between superficial motivations and soul-level reasons. You'll explore how to dig beneath the surface of your past experiences, emotional wounds, and inner drives to uncover the *real reason* you want more.

This isn't about goals.

It's about *fuel*.

Because when your why is strong enough, you don't need to push—you'll feel pulled.

Let's find that fire.

CHAPTER SIX

JUSTIFY YOUR WHY: THE LIES THAT KEEP YOU STUCK

"A superficial why can power a sprint, but only a deep why sustains a marathon."
—Simon Sinek

I REMEMBER SITTING ON THE EDGE OF MY COUCH, MY FOOT bouncing like a jackhammer. I had just turned down a deal that once would have seemed like everything I wanted. I was overwhelmed with anxiousness, and it felt like the air had been sucked out of the room. That's when I realized: I wasn't just making a decision—I was stepping into a new identity.

This chapter is about that moment. That choice. That why.

The most successful people I've met aren't chasing applause or dollars. They're pulled forward by something deeper—something they can't not do. Their why is a gravitational force that anchors their decisions and launches them into action, even on the worst days.

If you've made it this far, you're starting to feel that pull. You're not here just to tweak your career. You're here because something inside you is saying I was made for more.

Fighting for Loyalty and Justice

While creativity brought me joy, moments of struggle instilled in me a deep sense of loyalty and justice. In middle school, I struggled to connect until one friend brought me into his circle. That group became my family. We protected each other fiercely, and I carried that loyalty like a badge of honor.

I got into fights to defend them. Once, I punched a kid while wearing a cast because he hit someone I felt couldn't protect themselves. Loyalty was my way of showing up for others—the way I wished someone had shown up for me.

One incident stands out. My friends and I were caught lighting a fire where we shouldn't have. While two other kids involved got off easy, my best friend and I were labeled the "bad kids." His father, a former Marine and attorney, stood up for us at the disciplinary meeting. He didn't excuse our actions, but he demanded fairness. Watching him command the room left a profound impact on me. It showed me there was another way to fight—a way that used presence, voice, and truth. That moment became part of my why: to be someone's advocate, not just someone's defender.

The Struggles and Seeds of Possibility

Not all moments of struggle were as clear-cut. In high school, I had a teacher who gave me a grade on a test that didn't seem right. As he went through the answers, I realized he had marked correct responses as wrong. Frustrated, I called him an "asshole" and stormed out of the classroom.

I was sure I'd be expelled from my strict, all-boys private school. But instead, the dean of students—known for being tough—advocated for me behind closed doors. He saw the injustice in how the teacher treated me and gave me a second chance. That moment planted a seed in me. It wasn't just about justice; it was about possibility. Maybe I was more than what I saw in the mirror. Maybe I wasn't just a "C student." Maybe I could be something more.

From Struggle to Why

Your why is forged in friction—in moments you felt unseen, in times you wanted more, not just for yourself, but for others. For me, it started with the desire to protect people who didn't have a voice and evolved into building systems that empower them. It's not just about what I've overcome. It's about who I want to become—and what I want to help others become, too.

Motivational Drivers and Emotional Fuel

When you close your eyes, or when you talk to your spouse or closest friends, do you have a dream? Do you feel a pull toward something bigger than yourself? For me, it was always clear. I would tell everyone who would listen about my vision for the firm I wanted to build—a firm filled with inspiring leaders, where the team was united by a shared mission and inspired by a common vision. If you're reading this book, it's likely because something is calling to you, too.

Vision is essential—if you can't see it, it can never become a reality. Your why begins as a dream, a vision of what's possible, even if it feels just out of reach. Holding onto that dream and taking action to bring it to life allows you to set yourself on the path to achieving it.

Your why is often rooted in powerful, emotional moments— times when you realized the need for change or saw a bigger vision. These moments are what keep you connected to your deeper motivations, especially when challenges arise. Your why becomes the force that propels you to act. Without it, you risk living an empty, unfulfilled life.

There will always be voices telling you that you're crazy or reminding you of the percentage of businesses that fail. But remember, history is filled with entrepreneurs, like Steve Jobs, who were once seen as outlandish dreamers but ultimately changed the world. These leaders remained steadfastly committed to their why. That commitment gave them the drive to push through self-doubt and external resistance, keeping them focused on what truly matters.

The truth is, entrepreneurship is hard. The level of sacrifice required to build something meaningful is immense. But if that sacrifice is tied to a superficial why, it can lead to burnout, an early grave, and dying unfulfilled.

I didn't leave my nine-to-five over finances; I left because it didn't fulfill my why or my purpose. The paycheck and financial stability were there, but they weren't enough to keep me tethered to something that didn't align with who I wanted to be or what I wanted to create. I realized that true fulfillment comes from living in alignment with your why, not just achieving external markers of success. Without that alignment, even the biggest wins can feel hollow.

When your why is rooted deeply, you'll face challenges with a different perspective. You'll be willing to try and fail, knowing that you are exactly where you're supposed to be, rather than never trying and spending your life wondering what could have been. Your why gives you the courage to move forward, even in the face of uncertainty, to pursue a dream that feels authentic and true to your core.

It's important to understand that people don't hire companies; they hire individuals. And people don't align themselves with companies like Nike and Apple; they buy into their why. Nike's why is to "bring inspiration and innovation to every athlete in the world," defining everyone as an athlete. Apple's why is "to challenge the status quo and think differently," creating a culture around innovation and simplicity. These companies inspire loyalty because their why resonates on a deeper level. Customers aren't just buying products—they're aligning with a purpose.

I could have stayed in my job and been financially successful. But what would have been the point if I wasn't fulfilled? A nine-to-five paycheck might provide security, but it can never give you the kind of purpose that sustains you through challenges. If your why isn't meaningful—if it doesn't inspire you and align with your identity—you'll always feel like something is missing. Finding your why isn't just about building something; it's about building a life of purpose. It's about creating something that fills the void, that fuels you when times are tough, and that inspires you to keep moving forward, no matter the obstacles.

The Danger of a Superficial Why

A superficial why can fuel short-term wins, but it won't sustain you. Without deeper purpose, success leads to burnout, not fulfillment. I once spoke to someone starting a new venture who said, "If I don't make a million dollars in two years, I'll quit." That kind of mindset isn't sustainable because it's tied to a number, not a purpose. Without a meaningful why, success becomes a shell—shiny on the outside but empty inside. It may inspire envy, but it won't inspire *you*.

I had the financial success—but not the fulfillment. That's when I realized a paycheck without purpose is just a padded prison.

When I reflect on my own journey, I realize my initial why was limited. It was driven by a desire to prove others wrong and to be seen. That drive pushed me to work harder and achieve more, but it left me feeling empty. My deeper why, the one that now fuels me, is rooted in building, inspiring, and empowering others. It's not about proving anyone wrong; it's about creating something bigger than myself.

Building Your Golden Circle: Aligning Purpose with Action

In my journey to understand and justify my why, I've found a powerful framework that simplifies the process of aligning purpose with action. Inspired by Simon Sinek's concept of the

Golden Circle, this approach begins with identifying your core beliefs and builds outward to shape how you act and what you achieve. While Sinek's teachings laid the groundwork, I've adapted the framework to make it actionable for entrepreneurs navigating their own transformations.

At the heart of the Golden Circle are three key layers. The first is your why, which represents your core purpose or belief. It's not just a goal or mission—it's the deeply personal reason that drives your actions. For me, my why is to build, inspire, create, and revolutionize industries by fostering growth, empowerment, and innovation in others. On a personal level, my why is about living with purpose and integrity while inspiring my family and team to thrive. Defining your why is the most crucial step in any journey. Without a clear why, your efforts can feel aimless, and even success may feel hollow.

The second layer is your how, which represents the strategies, systems, and methods you use to bring your why to life. These are the deliberate steps that allow your purpose to manifest in tangible ways. For example, my how includes mentoring others, creating innovative systems, and cultivating a team culture that emphasizes both professional and personal growth. These actions align with my why and ensure my efforts are intentional and impactful.

Finally, there's your what, which is the tangible result of your why and how. This layer encompasses the products, services, or solutions you produce as a result of your purpose-driven efforts. For me, my what includes a thriving law firm built on innovation and trust, a med spa that empowers its clients and team members, and a legacy of businesses that challenge industry norms.

Starting with your why isn't just a theoretical exercise; it's a necessity. Too often, entrepreneurs jump straight to the what, focusing on products, revenue, or results without clarifying the deeper purpose driving those efforts. When you reverse the order and begin with your why, you create a foundation that shapes everything else. People don't connect with what you do; they connect with why you do it. Your why sets the tone for the story you tell, the culture you build, and the impact you create.

To see this in action, again, consider two of the most iconic brands in the world: Nike and Apple. Nike's why is "to bring inspiration and innovation to every athlete in the world." They define an athlete as anyone with a body, making their message inclusive and universally relatable. This purpose drives every campaign, every product, and every message they produce. When you buy a pair of Nike shoes, you're not just purchasing footwear; you're aligning yourself with their belief in personal potential and innovation.

Apple's why is equally powerful: "to challenge the status quo and think differently." Their purpose resonates with people who see themselves as innovators or rebels. Apple's products are more than devices; they're symbols of empowerment, simplicity, and creativity.

For entrepreneurs like you and me, applying this concept means building businesses that reflect our personal and professional values. When I established my law firm, my why wasn't about just winning cases; it was about creating an environment where my team could grow professionally and personally, where technology and trust worked hand in hand to serve clients better, and where collaboration redefined what a law firm could be. When I launched my med spa, my why wasn't just about offering services; it was about empowering my business partner, a stage 4 cancer survivor, to realize her vision and inspire others through her story. In both cases, my why became the guiding force that shaped every decision, from hiring team members to defining the culture and goals of the business.

When you lead with your why, you attract people who share your vision. This isn't just about clients or customers; it's about building a team, fostering partnerships, and creating relationships that align with your purpose. People don't connect to a product or service as much as they connect to the values behind it. When your why resonates, it inspires loyalty, trust, and enthusiasm that can't be manufactured.

While Simon Sinek's Golden Circle provides a clear structure, its true power lies in applying it to your unique journey. Start with your why and let it guide your how and what. Reflect on the deeper reasons you're pursuing your goals and ensure that everything you build is in alignment with that core purpose. Your why isn't just a motivational tool; it's the foundation for creating a life and business that are not only successful but also deeply fulfilling.

Ground yourself in your why. You'll move beyond superficial goals and external validation. You'll build something that not only drives success but also delivers the fulfillment and impact you've always envisioned. Your why will become the compass that keeps you on track, ensuring that every step you take is aligned with the legacy you're creating.

Letting go wasn't easy. But once I stopped chasing what looked good on paper, I began saying no to opportunities that didn't serve my vision. That's when I found true alignment—with a partner who shared my values and long-term mission.

Embracing Discomfort and Growth

Growth doesn't feel clean; it feels like chaos.

There came a moment when returning to my old life meant the slow death of my soul, but moving forward meant shedding the identity that once kept me safe.

I called an emergency therapy session and told my therapist, "I think I'm losing my mind."

She smiled and said, "Good. That means you're growing."

At the time, I hated her answer. But she was right.

Discomfort is not a red flag; it's proof you're evolving. You are not going backward. You're shedding.

It doesn't happen all at once. Growth is nonlinear. You might leap forward and then loop back. But with each loop, you're starting from a higher level.

That's why your why matters so much. When everything else feels unstable, your why becomes your anchor. It reminds you that this unraveling isn't failure—it's transformation.

Trusting the Process and Yourself

Trust each step, and trust that your why will carry you forward. Faith in yourself and the process sustains you through uncertainty. When you step into the new version of yourself, it can feel like unfamiliar territory because your authentic self often lives far beyond your autopilot self. You must have faith that the universe has your back and that by living by your why, you will carry out your purpose.

Setting Goals That Push Your Limits

Your goals should be bold enough to scare you. David Goggins, the renowned ultramarathon runner and motivational speaker, emphasizes setting goals that you don't think you can achieve because it's in the fear and discomfort that you grow. Goggins refers to this process as building your "mental resume"—a collection of proof points that show you are capable of far more than you believe.

When you've justified your why, you'll find the strength to push beyond your perceived limits. Your why provides the emotional and psychological fuel necessary to tackle goals that feel impossible.

I've experienced this firsthand. When I shifted from chasing superficial wins to living a purpose-driven life, my goals took on new meaning. It wasn't just about achieving for the sake of achievement anymore; it was about building, inspiring, and empowering. Knowing my why gave me the courage to take bold steps and set ambitious goals, even when I didn't have all the answers or guarantees of success.

Think of your why as the foundation for setting goals that challenge you to grow. Without it, fear and self-doubt might hold you back. With it, you'll have the clarity and motivation to embrace discomfort, knowing it's a necessary part of reaching your true potential.

Once you are clear on your why:

1. **Have a Vision of What You Want**
   Clarify the life you want to live and the impact you want to make. Write it down. I envisioned owning a firm, mentoring others, and creating systems and processes that would allow me to lead and build. I visualized working from anywhere in the world, having a team inspired by my vision, and creating opportunities for growth for my staff and myself.

2. **Create a Blueprint**
   Once you have the vision, break it into tangible steps. I knew I needed a certain amount of revenue, staff, and systems to support my vision. I identified what I needed to survive the transition financially and worked backward to create a detailed plan. Build it like it's already a reality.

3. **Commit to Consistent Action**
   Great businesses aren't built overnight—they're built through hard work and preparation. Before launching my firm, I spent years honing my craft, studying business, and preparing myself. Take the first step, no matter how small, and commit to the process.

4. **Be Willing to Shift as Needed**

   Goals evolve as you grow. My vision for my firm started as a referral-based business but shifted to include marketing and branding as I realized the need for sustainable growth. Allow room for evolution in your journey.

Your Why Is Only the Beginning

When your why is clear, the noise around you fades. You don't chase shiny distractions. You don't fold under pressure. You act with conviction.

But here's the truth: your why alone isn't enough.

If you don't examine the beliefs holding you back—if you don't rewrite the stories that tell you you're not ready, not worthy, not enough—then your why will stay buried under fear.

And so, in the next chapter, we'll uncover those limiting beliefs. Because your why deserves more than words. It deserves the freedom to breathe.

CHAPTER SEVEN

FROM VICTIM TO CREATOR: THE MINDSET THAT CHANGES EVERYTHING

Uncovering limiting beliefs is a necessary process, but get ready to be stripped of the world you know. When you change the lens through which you see reality, it can be unsettling and scary. That's what your beliefs do. They have the power to create or destroy. A belief is a practiced thought you have accepted as truth, so imagine what happens when that vision explodes in front of you. You've accepted these beliefs as reality, but in truth, they are merely the filters through which you experience life.

I struggled during this process and often felt ungrounded. There were times when I literally felt like I was going crazy, but that's where the magic happens. Uncovering and coming to terms with the fact that you don't live in the world—the world lives inside you—is both empowering and frightening. But it's in this shift that your life will completely change.

So, what does "the world lives inside you" mean? It means that everything you see, every experience you have, is filtered through your own perceptions, emotions, and beliefs. The same world that feels limitless to one person can feel suffocating to another, not because the world itself has changed but because of the lens through which it is viewed. Two people standing side by side can experience the same moment in completely different ways—one filled with fear and limitation, the other with possibility and hope. The difference isn't the external reality. It's the internal one.

This realization is both liberating and deeply confronting. It forces you to take responsibility. No longer can you blame external circumstances. No longer can you point to the world as the reason you feel small, unseen, or incapable. If the world you live in is simply a projection of your internal state, then the only way to change it is to change *you*.

And that is the moment of transformation. The moment when you stop reacting to the world as if it is something happening *to* you and start shaping it from the inside out. It's a life of empowerment, and it begins with the understanding that you are limitless. To own your life, you must own your beliefs. You have to confront the stories that have kept you stuck, seeing them for what they are—the old guard, brought in to protect a younger version of yourself. But now, that guard is exactly what's holding you back. I had to take off the Armor—the version of me that used output to hide from the truth. I had to let go of performance as identity and step into alignment as power. Only then could I move with real freedom.

Every day you stay hidden behind it, it drains you, slowly killing the potential within you. It's time to break free, to let go of a story that no longer serves you, and to choose a new reality. Because the truth is, the world you live in is nothing more than a reflection of what you believe it to be. Change the belief, and you change *everything*.

Generational Limiting Beliefs

Often, the voices of parents or loved ones become the echoes of our own limiting beliefs. They say things like *"Are you sure that's a good idea?"* or *"You should just be thankful for what you have."* These comments usually come from a place of love, not malice. They think they're protecting you, helping you avoid risks, or keeping you safe. But in reality, these well-intentioned words often reinforce the doubts you already carry.

Research underscores how generational beliefs shape our lives. A study in *Psychological Science* found that children internalize their parents' fears and attitudes by the age of seven, forming the foundation of their own decision-making and belief systems.[1] This process happens subconsciously—parents pass down their own limiting beliefs without even realizing it. For instance, parents who lived through financial hardship might teach their children to prioritize security over risk, instilling a fear of entrepreneurship or nontraditional career paths.

The *American Psychological Association* explains that phrases like *"Stick to what you know"* or *"Play it safe"* often reflect generational trauma rather than guidance tailored to the child's potential.[2] While these messages are designed to protect, they can unwittingly create a fear-based mindset—a mindset that locks us in velvet shackles.

My Personal Experience

My parents' fears were shaped by their own life experiences. During the 2008 financial crisis, my mom and dad lost money in the stock market, which made them skeptical of investing. My mom, the daughter of a stockbroker who worked a stable nine-to-five job, was raised with a traditional view of success: go to school, get a good education, and secure a reliable job. That was the lens through which she viewed the world, and it was the advice she passed down to me.

When I shared my plans to leave the firm, my dad's first reaction was concern: "Where are you going to get cases from?" My mom reminded me of my good salary, saying, "You make a good living." They weren't trying to discourage me; they wanted to protect me from the uncertainty that comes with entrepreneurship. But instead, I internalized their fears and used them to reinforce my own doubts. I thought, *What if I can't make it on my own? What if I fail?*

Breaking Free from the Lens of Others

Recognizing generational limiting beliefs means understanding that your loved ones' fears and perspectives don't have to define your truth. Their advice often comes from their own experiences, not yours. Their fears reflect their stories, not your potential.

Research supports the importance of questioning these beliefs. Research suggests that individuals who identify and reframe inherited beliefs or identity-based beliefs are more likely to pursue careers aligned with their passions.[3] Meanwhile, those who clung to fear-based beliefs often remained stuck in "safe" but unfulfilling roles.

Ask yourself, *Whose voice am I hearing when I feel doubt? Is this belief truly mine, or is it inherited?* Once you identify the origin of these beliefs, you can thank your loved ones for their concern while releasing their limitations. You can honor their love without adopting their fears.

The Freedom of Creating Your Own Lens

Breaking free from generational beliefs means creating your own lens. Yes, your parents and loved ones may want safety for you, but you can want growth, risk, and fulfillment for yourself. Their fears were never yours to carry—and now, you can finally let them go.

This process isn't about rejecting the love of your family. It's about understanding that their stories don't have to define your life. You can choose growth over safety, fulfillment over fear. When you let go of the beliefs you've inherited, you're finally free to create a vision for your life that's uniquely yours.

This is where the JUMP Method becomes a powerful tool in your transformation. It starts with deeply understanding *why* you need to take the leap in the first place. The pull toward something greater—whether it's freedom, purpose, or simply the need to know what you're capable of—must be stronger than the comfort of staying where you are. Without a strong enough reason, fear will always keep you tethered to the familiar.

But knowing your why isn't enough if you're still weighed down by old narratives. The stories you've been told—about security, success, and what is or isn't possible—shape your reality, often without you realizing it. To move forward, you have to uncover the limiting beliefs that keep you playing small. You have to recognize the inherited fears that whisper, *"Stay where it's safe,"* and challenge whether they were ever truly yours to begin with.

Growth requires a shift in mindset, one that allows you to see uncertainty not as a threat but as an opportunity. When you stop interpreting fear as a stop sign and start viewing it as a sign that you're stepping into expansion, everything changes. Instead of thinking, *What if I fail?* you begin asking, *What if this works?* Instead of clinging to the belief that safety is the goal, you start redefining success on your own terms.

And then comes the moment where belief turns into action. Taking the leap doesn't mean blindly jumping without a plan; it means building your wings as you go. Fear loses its grip when you commit to taking small, intentional steps forward. Each move, no matter how small, creates momentum, and momentum is what transforms a leap of faith into a calculated path toward something greater.

This is how you choose growth over safety and fulfillment over fear. You don't just wake up one day and shed the beliefs that have shaped you—you consciously rewrite them. You actively decide that the life you want is worth more than the comfort of staying where you are. The world doesn't hand you permission to go after it. You have to claim it for yourself.

And that's what the JUMP Method is all about: giving you the framework, the tools, and the belief that you don't have to live within the limits of the past. You get to decide. You get to create. You get to jump.

Those limiting beliefs didn't stay confined to my personal life—they showed up in my work, too. At the firm I worked for, recognition was rare. Wins were often met with pressure to do more or with silence. Conversations drifted toward luxury cars, vacations, and new houses—symbols of success—before snapping back to what we weren't doing well enough. It was disorienting. And at the time, I often found myself reacting defensively.

I've touched on this before—but here's what I hadn't yet realized: it also motivated me—for a while. But that motivation was rooted in proving I was good enough, chasing external validation from someone who simply didn't lead that way.

When you interpret everything through the lens of "I'm not good enough," and rely on external validation to feel fulfilled, even a boss pushing you to grow can feel like criticism—and trigger defensiveness instead of motivation.

When COVID hit and case volume plummeted, that pressure intensified. I began generating my own work, thinking that would finally silence the doubts. But instead of feeling proud or supported, I found myself fixating on offhand comments about money—comments I interpreted as questioning whether I deserved the success. One major win was scrutinized instead of celebrated—even as a competing firm courted the same case. But the real issue wasn't the case. It was the deeper belief I still carried: that I wasn't good enough to succeed on my own.

Eventually, the pressure that once fueled me began to wear me down—and forced me to confront the deeper issue.

So many high performers stay too long in environments that mirror their inner doubts—not because they're weak but because those doubts are familiar.

With time and distance, I came to see it differently. My boss wasn't the villain I had made him out to be—he was a businessman pushing for more. The story I had told myself filtered every interaction. I didn't see his drive as a push for growth; I saw it as proof that I wasn't measuring up. And instead of confronting the insecurity, I did what I had always done. I created distance and called it protection. But distance doesn't heal old beliefs. It only gives them more space to grow.

That realization changed everything. It was the moment I stopped trying to change other people and started challenging my beliefs about myself. If you've ever felt stuck, overwhelmed, or incapable, chances are, you're living under the weight of stories you didn't even realize you were carrying. But here's the good news: those stories aren't permanent.

Through this book, I'll show you how to uncover those limiting beliefs, challenge them, and break free. The Jump Method is designed to guide you step by step through this transformation. You'll learn how to identify the beliefs that are holding you back, how to rewrite them, and how to take bold action toward the life you've always wanted.

This isn't about staying stuck in reflection; it's about momentum. It's about clarity. It's about stepping into your power.

If I can do it, you can too.

Let's JUMP.

Shadow Work: Facing the Parts of Yourself You Avoid

Shadow work is the process of exploring the hidden, often disowned parts of yourself—the traits, emotions, or thoughts you've buried because they're uncomfortable to face. These shadows often manifest as projections, where you unconsciously attribute your own unacknowledged feelings or traits onto others. In doing so, you avoid taking responsibility for these parts of yourself, but the cost is steep: you stay stuck, unable to grow into your full potential.

Here's the truth: the things that frustrate or irritate you most in others often say more about you than about them. When you project, you're essentially holding up a mirror to yourself, revealing traits you've disowned or disapproved of in your own life. Shadow work helps you recognize these projections and, more importantly, reclaim the lessons they're trying to teach you.

I learned this from the incredible teachings of Debbie Ford and Janna Wilson, who guided me through shadow work principles and helped me uncover the deeper truths about myself. Their methods taught me that facing your shadow isn't about judgment; it's about compassion and curiosity.

For example, I always thought my boss was arrogant. The way he talked to me and others felt demeaning, and I often fired back at him. My frustration boiled over to the point that I even screamed at him and called him an asshole. I was lucky I was a high performer because there's no doubt I would have been fired otherwise—and rightfully so.

Looking back, I think it's fair to say that the person I am today would have fired my former self.

At the time, I believed my anger was justified, that he was the problem. But when I started to do shadow work, I realized something much deeper was happening. It wasn't his confidence I resented—it was my own lack of confidence. I saw his assertiveness as arrogance because I wasn't ready to embrace my own potential for leadership.

His behavior was a mirror, reflecting back the qualities I desperately needed to develop in myself. Once I recognized that, everything changed. I stopped viewing him as an adversary and started seeing him as a teacher. He wasn't the problem—he was the key to understanding my own insecurities and stepping into my own strength.

Steps to Begin Shadow Work

1. **Identify Triggers**
    Start by noticing the people or situations that irritate or frustrate you. Who makes your blood boil? What behaviors or traits do you find intolerable? Write these down without judgment.

2. **Ask, "What Does This Say About Me?"**
    For each trigger, ask yourself, *What about this person's behavior feels personal? Why does it bother me so much?* This step requires radical honesty. Often, you'll find that what annoys you in others is something you fear, reject, or desire in yourself.

3. **Trace the Origin**
    When did you first feel this way? Think back to moments in your past that might have planted the seed for this reaction. Did someone in your childhood embody this trait in a way that hurt or scared you? For me, my boss's confidence reminded me of my own insecurities from years of being told I wasn't good enough.

4. **Reframe the Trait**
    Once you've identified the projection, ask yourself, *How can I reclaim this trait as a strength?* For example, if you see someone as arrogant, could it mean you need to embrace your own confidence? If you judge someone for being overly emotional, could it mean you need to reconnect with your own feelings?

5. **Practice Self-Compassion**

   Shadow work can be uncomfortable, but it's essential to approach it with kindness. Remember, these traits aren't inherently bad; they're just parts of you that need acknowledgment and integration.

6. **Take Responsibility**

   Once you've identified and reframed your shadow, it's time to own it. Stop blaming others for what you see in yourself. Instead, thank them for revealing something you needed to address.

Why Shadow Work Matters

Shadow work isn't just about understanding your projections; it's about integration. When you reclaim the disowned parts of yourself, you become whole. You stop letting your triggers control you and start living from a place of empowerment.

I used to think my boss was the enemy, but he became one of my greatest teachers. He forced me to look inward, to confront the parts of myself I didn't want to see. That process didn't just change how I saw him—it changed how I saw myself.

The next time someone triggers you, pause and reflect. Ask yourself what that reaction reveals about you. What lesson is waiting to be learned? Because the truth is, your shadows aren't there to harm you; they're there to help you grow.

Reflection Prompt: Who Triggers You?

- Who triggers you the most in your life right now?
- What about them feels personal to you?
- What would it look like to reclaim that trait as a strength?

The Art of Forgiveness

Forgiveness isn't about letting someone off the hook for what they've done; it's about releasing the hold it has on you. It's about owning your circumstances and refusing to let past hurts define your future. The act of forgiveness frees you from the emotional weight that anchors you in anger, resentment, and blame. You can't be happy and angry at the same time. To create a life of fulfillment, you have to let go of what's holding you back. Forgiveness is the key to that freedom.

When you start working on limiting beliefs, you begin to see how much of people's actions come from their own stories and perspectives. Most people are acting in accordance with their belief systems, shaped by their experiences, and seeing the world through their own lens. This understanding doesn't excuse harmful behavior, but it allows you to step back and recognize that their actions are often a reflection of them, not you.

Adversity is an unavoidable part of life, but you get to choose how you react to it. Forgiveness is not a one-time act—it's a practice. It's a daily decision to release the emotional charge of what happened and shift your focus back to your growth and happiness.

I still struggle with forgiveness. For years, I didn't speak to my mom. I carried that pain and anger like armor, thinking it protected me, but all it did was weigh me down. Even now, I find myself getting angry when someone at work makes a mistake. But what I've learned is that these moments are mirrors—they show me what I still hold inside. When I feel frustration with someone else's failure, I have to ask myself, *How can I be fearless of failure if I can't allow those around me to fail?*

Forgiveness is about more than releasing others; it's about releasing yourself. When you practice the art of forgiveness, you open the door to forgiving your own mistakes. You give yourself the freedom to grow, to experiment, and to fail without fear. The more you let go of anger and resentment, the more space you create for joy, creativity, and connection. Mistakes aren't the end of the road—they're stepping-stones. Forgiveness allows you to embrace that truth.

Practical Steps to Cultivate Forgiveness

1. **Recognize the Emotional Cost**: Reflect on how holding onto anger or resentment affects your happiness. Ask yourself, *What is this grudge costing me?*
2. **Shift Your Perspective**: Try to see the situation from the other person's point of view. What belief systems or past experiences might have influenced their actions? This doesn't excuse their behavior, but it helps you depersonalize it.
3. **Forgive Yourself First**: Acknowledge your own mistakes and release the guilt or shame attached to them. Remember, failure is a part of growth, not a reflection of your worth.
4. **Create a Forgiveness Ritual**: Write a letter to the person you're forgiving—not to send but to express everything you need to let go of. Then destroy it as a symbolic act of release.
5. **Practice Gratitude**: Shift your focus from what hurt you to what you've learned from the experience. What growth has come from this adversity?
6. **Stay Consistent**: Forgiveness is a process, not a single event. Each time the anger resurfaces, remind yourself of your commitment to let it go.

Forgiveness isn't just about others; it's about you. It's about creating emotional space for happiness, fulfillment, and growth. When you forgive, you stop letting past hurts dictate your present. You take back control of your life and step into the role of the creator, shaping your reality with intention and purpose. Forgiveness doesn't erase adversity, but it transforms how you move through it.

As you embrace forgiveness, you'll find yourself letting go of perfection, both in yourself and others. You'll stop fearing mistakes and start seeing them as opportunities for growth. Forgiveness is the bridge between anger and joy, between fear and love, and between stagnation and transformation. It's not easy, but it's worth it.

The art of forgiveness is one of the greatest tools for creating a life of freedom, resilience, and peace. It's the foundation for releasing the past, embracing the present, and building the future you deserve.

Identifying Limiting Beliefs

Limiting beliefs are the quiet voices in your mind that whisper, "You're not good enough," "This isn't for people like you," or "You'll never succeed." Living from a self-limiting story confines what you're capable of achieving. These stories may cause you to give up on everything your soul craves just because remaining the victim of your narrative feels easier and more comfortable.

Most of these stories were formed early in life, often by a wounded part of you—a younger self who felt hurt, rejected, or small. In response, you created a story to protect yourself—a way to survive in a world that felt uncertain and threatening.

You can identify your limiting beliefs by paying attention to the emotions that surface when you think about taking bold action or making a significant change. That emotion is where the story lies, the one holding you in place. Often, this feeling can be traced back to painful moments in childhood—times when you felt utterly defeated or accepted a distorted reality as the truth, or even moments that seemed insignificant at the time but left a mark.

Take a moment to think back to when you first felt that familiar pang of doubt or fear. What was happening? This won't be easy, as it means confronting past trauma, but understand that this difficult journey is the only way to break free from the confines of the world you've created for yourself. Close your eyes and breathe slowly—in through your nose and out through your mouth. Confronting these stories can be deeply painful, and often, the more intense the moment, the stronger and more limiting the belief. But remember, the only way out is through.

The beliefs you created in these moments have gone unquestioned for years. They served a purpose once, but now, they're just barriers that keep you from truly living. This is the moment to face them head-on, to question and release the stories that no longer serve you.

My Family and the Beliefs I Carried

I grew up in a big family but spent a lot of time alone. My siblings were tough on me; they teased me relentlessly, and I internalized it all. I vividly remember being left alone in public places whenever I cried, even as a small child. My family's approach to emotion was clear: it wasn't acceptable. I can still see myself hiding in a clothes rack, tears streaming down my face, wondering if they would ever come back for me.

That dynamic extended beyond my immediate family. My mom's side of the family was huge, and the competitive nature of it was undeniable. Cousins were compared like trophies, and I often felt like I wasn't measuring up. My aunts would tease me for being disorganized and forgetful. To me, those words confirmed what I feared most—that I wasn't good enough.

These experiences shaped the belief that I didn't matter and that I wasn't capable. As a teenager, I fled from my family, spending most of my time at friends' houses or living in a property my dad was renovating. My inner dialogue was brutal, and I convinced myself that success was the only way to prove I mattered. This belief drove me relentlessly, but it also left me empty, even as I achieved more than I ever thought possible. I didn't realize it then, but my high performance had become my armor. I wasn't just working hard; I was defending myself with achievement. It felt like ambition, but really, it was protection. That's what I now call High Performer's Armor—overachievement as a defense mechanism. Output became my proof of worth.

Limiting Beliefs → Internal Scripts

These are the subconscious narratives you've absorbed that now filter your reality.

You're not broken. You're just living by an outdated internal script.

The Framework to Uncover and Transform Limiting Beliefs

Changing your life starts with understanding and transforming your beliefs. Here's a framework to guide you:

1. Acknowledge the Pain Points

Start by identifying the areas in your life where you feel dissatisfied or stuck. These areas often point to a deeper belief system that is holding you back. Take a moment to reflect on your internal dialogue in these situations. What do you hear yourself saying? Perhaps it's, "I'm not good enough," "I don't deserve success," or "This isn't for people like me." Write these down. Be brutally honest with yourself. These are the beliefs you need to confront.

2. Trace the Origin of the Belief

Once you've identified a limiting belief, dig deeper. Where did it come from? Start by going back to the emotion you feel when you tell yourself you can't do something. Sit with that feeling and ask yourself, *When have I felt this way before?* Let your mind take you back to moments in your past that planted the seed of this belief. Was it something someone said to you? A failure you experienced? A childhood event that made you feel small or unworthy?

These moments might include being dismissed by a teacher, feeling overlooked by a parent, or failing in a way that left a lasting scar. Often, these beliefs started as a way to protect yourself, a coping mechanism to survive difficult moments. But now, they've become chains holding you back. Recognizing their origin allows you to see them for what they truly are—stories, not truths. Acknowledge their roots so you can start letting them go.

3. Build Your Mental Resume

Now, it's time to challenge those beliefs with hard evidence. Start by listing your accomplishments—every goal you've achieved, every obstacle you've overcome, and every time you've proven yourself capable. Write them down. This is your mental resume, a tool to counteract the doubts and insecurities that hold you back. When limiting beliefs creep in, return to this list. Let your achievements remind you of your resilience, resourcefulness, and ability to succeed. Your mental resume becomes a living testament to the truth: you are capable.

But let's be honest—**when you're in it**, it's hard to see it that way.

You don't feel strong. You feel cracked open. Exposed.

A mentor of mine once told me something I'll never forget:

"Healing isn't a destination. It's a practice."

The same goes for how you view your story.

It's not a one-time rewrite.

It's a daily decision.

To pick up the lens again.

To stop judging the pain.

To hold space for the full truth.

And to start seeing the gifts buried inside it.

That's what happened for me.

My wife and I had been trying to get pregnant for years. We saw doctors. Held onto hope. Faced disappointment over and over.

And for a long time, I didn't see how *my own story* was part of what needed healing.

But when I finally leaned into the discomfort—when I chased what I was really called to do, when I stopped pretending I was okay and started treating myself and my past with the respect they deserved—something shifted.

We got pregnant.

And not just with a child but with possibility. With purpose.

Our daughter Noah was born during the same season I was finally becoming who I really am.

Her name means *rest* and *comfort*—which is exactly what she brought into a life that had been driven, anxious, and uncertain for so long.

But it's also the name of a man who trusted the storm. Who built something when it made no sense to build. Who believed something better was coming on the other side.

At the time, my older daughter—just seven years old—had one quiet fear:

Would this new season mean I'd have less time with her?

What actually happened, as it so often does when you honor your truth, is the opposite.

I've spent more time with her than ever. We've forged a deeper bond. More presence. More laughter. More connection.

That's the practice: **to see the story clearly and still look for the gift it came to give you.**

Sometimes, the gift is more beautiful than anything you ever could have planned.

Reflection Prompt: Identifying Your Strengths and Gifts

What part of your story have you judged as weakness … that might actually hold your greatest strength?

What gift might be waiting for you on the other side of honoring your truth?

Empower Your Stories!

We can all find ourselves stuck in trauma competitions, where our addiction to pain becomes the defining narrative of who we are. It's easy to let your trauma feel like the thing that makes you unique, the thing that separates you from others. For a long time, I used my tough times as excuses to stay stuck, to play small.

But here's what I've learned: your traumas aren't meant to define you—they're meant to teach you. They reveal your capacity to endure, to grow, to fight, and to become. I have had tough times in my life, and for a while, I let them hold me back. But when I finally faced them, I realized they were all beautiful lessons, shaping me into the person I am today.

We must stop glorifying the struggle and start using it.

Empower the wound. Don't wear it like a badge of identity— channel it like fuel for your next creation. Your story isn't proof that you're broken; it's proof that you're still building. Pain may shape you, but it doesn't have to brand you.

Even the loss of my father, who became my best friend later in life, has become a beautiful moment for me. His death was a reminder of everything I have to live for. I'll never forget him looking at me and saying, "I don't know where I'm going, but I can't imagine it being better than here." He said this as he sat in bed, unable to walk, fresh off a ventilator, living in my brother's basement after my mom had left him a couple of years earlier.

And yet, he still had so much love for life.

That moment changed me. He may have been scared of his mortality, but what I learned was that his soul was immortal and that the legacy we leave lives on in the people we pass it down to. I told myself for years that I didn't know how I would live without him. His loss forced me to confront my broken relationship with my mother and my fractured ties with other members of my family. It reminded me to wake up and truly live, to forgive, and to embrace everything that is magical about my existence.

Take Viktor Frankl, for example. Frankl was a psychiatrist and Holocaust survivor. He lost his family in concentration camps, endured unimaginable suffering, and lived through horrors that most of us can't even comprehend. Frankl could have succumbed to despair, bitterness, and the belief that life was meaningless. Instead, he found profound purpose in his suffering. He realized that while he couldn't control his circumstances, he could control how he responded to them.

This understanding became the foundation of his groundbreaking book, *Man's Search for Meaning*, which has inspired millions of people to find purpose, even in the darkest moments. Frankl's story is the ultimate testament to how even the most devastating experiences can reveal strength and purpose we never knew we had.

I'm genuinely thankful for all my struggles—every moment of rejection, every failure, every setback. Without them, I wouldn't be me. They taught me resilience, self-reliance, and strength. They showed me my capacity to push beyond what I thought possible.

Embrace the Pain

Embrace what life throws at you. Let it teach you what you're capable of. You're stronger than you know, and the adversity you face is preparing you for the incredible life waiting on the other side.

Your pain isn't a reason to stop—it's a reason to keep going. It's not the end of your story; it's the fuel for the next chapter. The moment you decide to stop being addicted to your trauma and instead use it to transform, you'll discover that your deepest struggles can become your greatest strengths.

Take a moment to reflect:

- What tough experiences have shaped you into who you are today?
- What would it mean to look at those moments not as burdens but as gifts?

Embrace the lessons. Use them as a foundation to build the life you're meant to live.

Your story isn't your excuse—it's your edge.

Finding and Shifting Limiting Beliefs: A Path to Transformation

The life you're living isn't just the result of outside forces; it's shaped by the beliefs you carry about yourself and the world around you. Your reality reflects the stories you've repeated, the truths you've accepted, and the fears you've internalized. Some of those beliefs protect you. Others quietly imprison you.

But here's the truth: beliefs are not facts. They're patterns. And patterns can be rewritten.

See the Story You're Living

Transformation begins with awareness. You can't shift what you're unwilling to see.

For years, I told myself I was chasing success because I wanted to be excellent. But when I looked closer—really looked—I realized I was chasing it to prove something. To quiet a voice that said I wasn't good enough. To outrun the shame of being underestimated. That belief, buried under layers of drive and productivity, had shaped everything. It was the hidden lens coloring every goal and relationship.

The moment I saw the story, I could start to rewrite it.

You don't have to believe everything you think. If your inner voice says, "I'm not smart enough," "I don't belong," or "I'll always struggle," pause. Ask: "Is this truth—or just a well-practiced thought?" Awareness creates space. Space creates choice. That's where power begins.

Adopt a Growth Lens

The biggest lie that limiting beliefs whisper is that who you are now is all you'll ever be.

But I've seen firsthand that identity is fluid, especially when you decide to stretch. A fixed mindset says, "I can't." A growth lens reframes it: "I can learn." It doesn't mean you'll never struggle. It means you won't stop there.

Your past isn't a prophecy. It's a pattern—until you interrupt it. You've already proven this. Every time you learned something hard or overcame a challenge, you created evidence that your story could change. Let that fuel you.

Rewriting the Narrative

The moment you choose to believe you are capable, deserving, and ready—even if you don't fully feel it yet—you start building a new identity.

That's not delusion. It's direction.

Visualizing who you want to become isn't about fantasy— it's about focus. It gives your brain a target. When you start acting like the future version of you, you begin closing the gap between who you've been and who you're becoming.

Ask yourself, *If I already believed I was enough, what would I do next?*

Then do that.

Change Your State

When fear takes over, your body joins the story. Shoulders tense. Breathing shortens. Your posture caves. You shrink into the belief.

But you can shift your state—and with it, your story.

Move. Breathe. Walk. Stretch. Speak out loud. Change your environment. Break the physical pattern to loosen the mental one. This isn't a hack. It's a reminder that you don't have to wait to "feel better" before you take control. Action changes identity. State changes belief.

Your Daily Rewiring Practice

Rewiring limiting beliefs is not about waiting for some perfect moment of clarity. It's about consistent, imperfect action, like:

- **Starting small**: Pick one thought that holds you back. Write it down. Then challenge it.
- **Taking one bold action**: Ask, *What would I do if I already believed I was worthy?* Then move in that direction.
- **Rehearsing your truth**: Repetition reprograms. Speak your new belief daily until it feels more real than the old one.

Commit to Uncovering Limiting Beliefs All Along Your JUMP Journey

Just remember:

1. **Beliefs Create Reality**
   If you think you can't, your brain will find proof that you can't. If you think you can, it will also find

proof of that. Your belief sets the boundaries of your potential.

2. **Your Story Is Editable**
   You're not bound to the script your childhood or past experiences wrote for you. You can be the author now.

3. **Your Past Holds Fuel, Not Chains**
   What once limited you can now become your launchpad—if you choose to reframe it.

4. **Align with Purpose**
   When you know your "why," even hard things have meaning. Purpose quiets fear.

5. **Act Before You're Ready**
   Action creates belief. Don't wait to feel brave—move, and the courage will catch up.

6. **Repetition Builds Belief**
   The stories you repeat shape your identity. Make sure they serve you.

7. **You Are the Author Now**
   Your future isn't waiting for permission. It's waiting for your decision.

Reflection Prompt: What Belief About Success or Failure Is Keeping You Safe but Small?

Journal a story you've repeated since childhood. Then rewrite it from an empowered lens.

Once you've named your fears and rewritten your story, it's time to build the runway …

CHAPTER EIGHT

MINDSET IS THE RUNWAY

MINDSET IS THE THIRD STEP OF THE JUMP METHOD—AND THE ground you build before you lift. Your beliefs drive your behavior, your behavior sets your results, and your results reinforce your beliefs. If those beliefs are borrowed from conformity, they'll keep you parked at the gate. Think of your runway as something you build before takeoff—emotionally, spiritually, and yes, financially. One of the most practical ways to begin is through "runway journaling": a daily, five-minute practice where you write down the fears that hold you back, the beliefs that keep you grounded, and the vision that pulls you forward. The more honest you get, the clearer your next steps become. Your mindset isn't just a feeling; it's something you train, one page at a time.

Because mindset is more than a mental upgrade—it's your runway.

Before a plane ever takes off, it needs solid ground, alignment, and acceleration. The runway is where momentum is built, vision is clarified, and lift becomes possible. Without one, you're just falling out of the sky. With it, you fly with purpose and direction.

Mindset is your runway. It's the stretch of emotional, financial, and spiritual preparation that gives your jump power. It's how you build belief when you don't yet have results. It's what keeps you steady when the old system tugs at you to stay small. Without this foundation, you don't leap—you flail. With it, you take off.

That's why we build it first. Before the leap. Before the business plan. Before the outcome. The runway is the inner shift that turns a blind jump into a bold launch.

The System That Keeps You Stuck

You have been told the formula for success: get an education, take on debt, climb the corporate ladder, and hope that, one day, your retirement will be enough to enjoy what's left of life. But let's be honest—this path was built for security, not freedom. And for an entrepreneur, that simply isn't enough.

This formula doesn't teach you to think beyond your paycheck, to envision a life of limitless potential, or to navigate the bold, unpredictable world of entrepreneurship. It's a system designed to keep you comfortable, compliant, and contained—a framework that prioritizes stability over growth and discourages risk in favor of routine. For those who feel called to create, to build, and to forge their own path, this system doesn't just fall short—it stifles.

If you don't challenge this system, it will quietly consume your ambition. Every "yes" to the wrong thing—be it another task, another opportunity, or another safe choice—further cements the life you don't want. Breaking free requires learning when to say no.

If You Don't Break Free

If you don't break free from this script now, you risk waking up one day, staring into the mirror, and wondering where your dreams went. The routine that once felt safe can become the slow erosion of your passion, your purpose, and the life you were meant to live. The slow death of an unfulfilled soul is the most profound kind of death—a quiet whisper of regret that grows louder with every passing year.

But the system doesn't have to define you. Unless you've inherited an empire, you have to build one. And it starts with a decision—not a fleeting thought but a bold, unwavering commitment to a new way of life.

Decisions create momentum. that people who make firm,

intentional decisions are not only more successful but also more fulfilled.[4] Every transformation begins with that single, pivotal choice to step off the path of least resistance and create something uniquely yours.

Say No to Say Yes

You have to say no to the wrong opportunities to say yes to the right ones. Every time you say yes to something that doesn't align with your vision, you're saying no to your dream. It's easy to make decisions out of fear—fear of failure, fear of the unknown, fear of rejection. But those fear-based decisions will never lead you to the life you truly want.

Often, people struggle to say no. Think about areas in your life where you find it difficult. I was that person, and I know how it feels. I used to never say no to more work, to people asking me for favors, or to anyone needing something from me. I was the guy who always said yes. The truth is, it wasn't out of generosity; it was rooted in fear. Fear of rejection, fear of not being liked, and ultimately, the belief that I wasn't good enough. Saying yes to everything felt like a way to prove my worth, but in reality, it only drained me and pulled me further from my vision.

Every yes made out of fear is a quiet no to your future.

If you relate to this, start small. The next time you're asked for something, don't respond right away. Simply say, "Let me think about it." Give yourself space to sit with what's being asked of you. Ask yourself, *Am I agreeing to this out of fear? What fear is driving this decision?* Are you afraid you won't be successful if you say no? Are you afraid you won't be liked? Where does that fear come from?

This process is a critical part of the **Mindset Shift**. When you pause to reflect before responding, you begin to rewire the automatic, fear-based patterns that have kept you stuck. Shifting your mindset requires breaking free from reactive decisions and embracing intentionality. This simple act of saying, "Let me think about it," is a way of reclaiming your power, allowing you to approach decisions with clarity and confidence rather than fear.

Mindset shifts happen in these small, everyday moments. As you practice identifying fear and choosing alignment instead, you'll begin to see how changing your thought patterns leads to transformative actions. This is how you create a new reality— one choice at a time.

Often, the root of this fear lies in childhood. Many of us made unconscious agreements as children, believing that to be loved, we had to please others, meet expectations, or never disappoint. These agreements shape how we interact with the world as adults. But as adults, we have the power to rewrite those agreements. We can choose to make decisions based on authenticity and vision rather than fear or pressure.

When I started my firm, I had to say no to offers that, on the surface, seemed promising. Firms offered me leadership roles, partnerships, and lucrative paychecks. But every one of those offers came with strings that would tie me to someone else's vision. Saying no wasn't easy, but it was necessary.

Then, one day, my current law partner approached me with a merger opportunity. At the time, I didn't know him well, but for some reason, it didn't matter. I knew his reputation and could tell the type of person he was after our first interaction. There was a sense of trust and alignment that I hadn't felt with other offers.

It wasn't an easy decision; it stirred up the same fear and uncertainty I'd faced before. But this time was different—it aligned with my vision. At that stage, my focus was on acquiring cases, and I hadn't yet built the strong systems and processes we'd eventually need. He was a great trial lawyer with an exceptional team behind him, and together we saw the potential to create something far greater than either of us could have achieved alone. Saying no to the wrong opportunities in the past allowed me to say yes to this one, and that decision changed everything. It was a moment of clarity, where fear gave way to alignment, and the result was a partnership built on shared values, trust, and a vision for growth.

Warren Buffett said it best: "The difference between successful people and really successful people is that really successful people say no to almost everything." Saying no isn't about arrogance or selfishness; it's about clarity. This is where the first step of the JUMP Method, **Justify Your Why**, comes back into focus.

When you remember your "why," you guard it fiercely. Your "why" becomes your compass, helping you make decisions that align with your vision and values. Saying no to the wrong opportunities isn't a rejection; it's an act of protecting your purpose and creating space for the right ones. The more intentional you are in saying no, the more room you have for the opportunities that truly matter and move you closer to your goals.

When we act out of fear, we are trying to control our environment. As children, control made us feel safe. But as adults, the greatest gifts in life are often found in the unknown. Saying no to fear-based decisions creates space for authentic, aligned opportunities to find you. It's not about rejection; it's about creating room for what truly matters.

Reflection Prompt:
What Are You Saying Yes To?

- What are you currently saying yes to that doesn't align with your vision?
- What would saying no to those things make space for in your life?

The Creator Versus the Victim

Life will test you—it always does. What determines the outcome is how you choose to respond. The victim believes life is happening *to* them. To them, every challenge is a personal attack, every setback a sign that they are powerless. They see the world as an unforgiving force that dictates their circumstances, and in that perspective, they find an excuse to stay stagnant.

The creator, on the other hand, understands that life is happening *for* them. Every setback is not the end but a setup for something greater. They embrace turbulence because they know it's not something to fear; it's a force that shakes them awake, clears **the Fog**, and reveals the path they couldn't see before.

The victim mindset can feel safe because it removes accountability. When everything is someone else's fault—such as the economy, your upbringing, your boss—you can avoid the hard work of change. But that comfort comes at a steep price: stagnation. Every day spent in the victim mindset is a day where potential is wasted, dreams are delayed, and transformation is stalled.

Here's the hard truth: the moment you pass blame, you are telling the world that someone else has control over your life. If someone told you that you can't do something, and you let that stop you, then they control you. If you allow circumstances, people, or opinions to dictate your actions, you've given away your power. The only way out is to take it back.

It's completely normal to feel upset and frustrated by your circumstances—those emotions are a natural response to struggle. They don't make you weak or unworthy; they make you human. But the key is to not let those emotions define you or your path forward. You have to move through them, not around them, knowing that they're temporary and that on the other side is growth and something greater waiting for you.

You have to own your life, own your problems, and own your struggles. The creator mindset demands that you take full ownership of everything—your wins and your failures—because they are all part of your growth. The world isn't working against you; it's guiding you, pushing you, and challenging you to rise. But here's the catch: what you resist will persist. If you fight against reality, you'll stay stuck in it. But when you allow it—when you stop resisting the lessons, the turbulence, and the challenges—then, and only then, can it direct you toward something greater. This is the turning point: when you empower the wound.

That means choosing not to let pain define you but to let it refine you. The wound isn't your brand—it's your breakthrough. If you're stuck in struggle, it's not because of the pain; it's because you've mistaken it for your identity. Embracing the discomfort, facing it head-on, is what transforms it into a stepping-stone instead of a roadblock.

Embracing Ownership

The creator mindset is about ownership and responsibility. The creator recognizes that while they can't control everything, they can always control how they respond. They lean into the discomfort of turbulence, knowing it's within these moments of chaos that transformation begins. They don't see failure as final. Instead, they see it as feedback, a step toward growth. Every misstep is a teacher, every challenge a chance to rise stronger.

Psychologist Martin Seligman's research on learned helplessness illustrates this perfectly. When people are repeatedly exposed to challenges without a sense of control, they learn to give up. But the creator refuses to surrender. They take back their power by owning their decisions, reframing struggles as opportunities, and shifting their perspective from limitation to possibility. They know that their stories shape their reality, so they tell better stories.

One of the most powerful lessons in shifting from a victim to a creator mindset is understanding the concept of duality. Success and failure aren't opposites; they're part of the same journey. You cannot grow without challenges, just as you cannot appreciate light without experiencing darkness. The creator loves turbulence because they know the lessons it brings are what shape them. The shake isn't something to avoid; it's the wake-up call that helps you see the path more clearly.

Duality teaches us that both the highs and lows of life are valuable. Success may fill you with pride, but failure teaches resilience. Wins build momentum, but losses build strength. When you embrace this truth, you stop fearing failure because you realize it's not the end; it's a part of the process. As a creator, you learn to find meaning in both.

Your decisions define the reality you create. But here's the catch: indecision is also a decision—a decision to remain stuck, to avoid discomfort, to stay in the safety of inaction. The creator mindset demands courage. To reclaim your power, you must decide to move forward, even when the path isn't clear. Life doesn't wait for you to feel ready. Transformation begins the moment you say, "I am ready to own my life."

Leaning into Turbulence

Turbulence is often misunderstood. To the victim, it feels like chaos, something to run from. But the creator knows that turbulence is the catalyst for growth. It's in the shake, the moments that disrupt your comfort zone, that you see what you're truly capable of. It's in those moments that clarity emerges, hidden strengths surface, and new opportunities appear.

Consider this: the most resilient and successful individuals are not the ones who avoid turbulence but the ones who embrace it. They welcome the discomfort, knowing it will reveal lessons they couldn't learn any other way. For the creator, turbulence isn't a roadblock—it's a guide.

The victim mentality is a lonely and dark place to live. When it feels like the world is stacked against you, you're left feeling powerless, trapped in a never-ending state of fight-or-flight. I spent most of my time fighting—swinging at the air, reacting to every blow life threw my way—but never really focusing on the target.

In that state, everything feels urgent, overwhelming, and unfair. It's exhausting, like running on a treadmill that never stops. No matter how hard you push, you can't seem to get ahead. But the problem with swinging at the air is that it doesn't accomplish anything—it's all effort, no direction.

For years, I stayed in a job, telling myself that if my boss could just see what I saw—if he could just understand what I was capable of—then I'd surely own the firm one day. I tied my hopes, my future, and my potential to someone else's vision, waiting for them to recognize what I could bring to the table. But they never did. When I finally mustered the courage to leave, I faced an unexpected blow: the firm took my phone number—the one I'd used as my primary means of communication for twelve years. I knew it was their number, but it still felt like my lifeline had been severed. How would people contact me now?

Not long after, my dad was rushed to the ICU. An emergency text was sent to my old number—the one I no longer had access to. I was promised those messages would be forwarded, but they weren't. In the chaos, I missed out on one of the last opportunities I would have had to see my dad alive.

At first, I was stuck in the role of the victim. I kept replaying the same thoughts: *Why would they take the number? Why didn't they send those messages?* But over time, I realized that replaying the past wasn't going to change it. The only way forward was to take ownership of my circumstances and ask myself, *What can I do next?*

The truth was, the phone number belonged to the firm. I had relied on it for over a decade without creating a backup plan. Losing those two days with my dad didn't define our relationship; it made me that much more intentional and present every time I saw him after that.

Grief visited again when a key team member passed, but her influence lived on in how we led. Even loss became a teacher in ownership.

The Shift from Victim to Creator Isn't Immediate

I left my firm because I was learning to own my circumstances, but even after I left, I found myself battling the same tired, old mindset I thought I had left behind.

The first couple of months were the hardest. I kept replaying the past, wondering what might have been different if things had gone my way, and feeling the pull of old habits—blaming, reacting, and swinging at the air without focus. Even though I had taken the leap to start building something new, part of me was still tied to the familiar struggles of the past.

I used to get so angry that I would push myself beyond measure—but with no direction. I'd run through walls only to get slammed in the head with a baseball bat. It was pure effort without purpose, and I stayed stuck in the cycle, frustrated and exhausted.

But now? I'm the f***ing bat. I own everything about my circumstances. Every hit, every challenge, every obstacle—they're mine to control.

I don't swing blindly anymore; I strike with intention.

I choose what matters and move with force, whether it's

negotiating a deal, building scalable systems, or coaching some-one through the same leap I once took. I don't burn energy trying to prove anything. I conserve it for impact.

Taking ownership means I'm no longer reacting to life—I'm creating it. And when you step into that mindset, nothing can stop you.

This moment represents more than just ownership; it's the shift from wild effort to surgical execution.

"I'm the f*****ing bat**" means you no longer waste energy swinging at everything. You choose your targets. You strike with precision. You control outcomes with clarity. You don't just reclaim your power—you wield it.

That's the difference between reacting and leading. That's the difference between surviving and building.

Shifting from victim to creator is a process. In the beginning, you have to consciously remind yourself to take ownership. It's about catching those old thoughts as they creep in and asking, *What can I own in this moment? What action can I take to move forward?*

The victim mentality isn't just lonely—it's paralyzing. But the moment you take responsibility, you reclaim your power. That's the shift—from swinging at the air to finally hitting your mark.

Practical Steps to Shift from Victim to Creator

1. **Reframe Your Challenges**: The next time you face a setback, pause. Ask yourself, *What lesson is hidden here? How can this experience shape me into a stronger, wiser version of myself?*

2. **Own Your Story**: Reflect on the narratives you've been telling yourself. Are they empowering or limiting? Rewrite your story to focus on your strengths and opportunities.

3. **Detach From Others' Energy**: Stop allowing your mood and actions to be dictated by others' emotions or circumstances. Ask yourself, *What is truly mine to own? What is theirs to carry?*

4. **Decide to Act**: Each day, make one small decision that aligns with your vision, no matter how uncomfortable it feels. Action, no matter how small, creates momentum.

5. **Shift Your Perspective**: When turbulence arises, remind yourself that it's not happening *to* you—it's happening *for* you. Practice gratitude for the growth it brings.

6. **Celebrate Resilience**: At the end of each day, reflect on a moment where you leaned into discomfort or took ownership of a challenge. Celebrate these small victories—they are proof of your transformation.

On Having Faith

Faith isn't about religion; it's about trust. Faith is believing in your ability to create a better future, even when the road ahead feels uncertain. It's about knowing, deep in your soul, that life is working in your favor. Without faith, the jump becomes a free fall. With faith, the jump becomes a flight.

To live with faith is to live on the edge. True courage isn't the absence of fear but the willingness to step into the unknown. Living on the edge doesn't mean being reckless; it means trusting that growth, transformation, and fulfillment exist when you're willing to leave the comfort zone and walk the line between fear and freedom. It's about believing that when you take the leap, the universe will meet you halfway. Faith isn't passive; it's the foundation of the creator's journey. It's what allows you to trust the turbulence, embrace the shake, and see challenges as part of the process rather than obstacles.

Faith doesn't just live in bold leaps; it shows up in the quiet, brutal conversations behind closed doors.

I remember sitting at the kitchen table, staring at numbers that didn't add up, trying to find the right words to explain to my family why we had to cut back. Not because we were careless but because I was betting on something that hadn't paid off yet. I had chosen this path. I had made this leap. And now, we all had to feel the free fall.

I had to look my wife in the eyes and say, "We're going to need to hold off on that trip … the house project … the comfort we're used to." Not because I didn't want to give her everything but because I was building something that demanded everything from me first.

And the harder conversation? The one I had with myself. Sitting alone, doing the math, wondering if I was delusional. Watching my bank account shrink and hearing the quiet voice of doubt creep in: What if this doesn't work?

But here's the thing—faith isn't the absence of doubt. It's choosing to move forward anyway. It's looking uncertainty in the face and saying, "I believe in what I can't yet see."

In those moments—when logic screams no, when fear makes your chest tighten—you don't need perfect clarity. You just need the next step. Faith fills in the rest.

Without faith, it's easy to fall back into the victim mindset, believing the world is working against you instead of for you. Faith shifts your perspective and opens the door for transformation.

When you embrace faith, everything begins to shift. The people around you change. Opportunities begin to align. Doors you didn't even know existed start to open. Faith brings clarity because it allows you to focus on what matters most: your vision. But it requires you to let go of needing certainty and control and instead trust in your vision and the process. Faith is what allows you to move forward, even when the path ahead feels unclear.

The reticular activating system (RAS) in your brain plays a crucial role in this process. The RAS filters what you notice in your environment, highlighting information that aligns with your beliefs and expectations. If you focus on scarcity and failure, your brain will show you evidence to support those beliefs. But when you focus on abundance, opportunity, and success, your RAS begins to find the people, resources, and solutions that align with your vision. Faith activates this system, training your brain to seek out the pathways to your goals.

Living on the Edge with Faith

When I decided to start my firm, I had no guarantees. I could have stayed in the comfort of what I knew—working in someone else's system, following someone else's rules. But I trusted in my vision. I believed that even without certainty, the jump was worth it. That leap of faith didn't just change my career—it changed my life. It brought the right opportunities, the right people, and the right lessons into my path. None of it would have happened if I had waited for certainty. Faith is what allowed me to act in the face of fear and uncertainty.

Faith requires action. It asks you to trust your decisions, your intuition, and your vision, even when doubt surrounds you. But here's the truth: faith isn't blind. It's built through practice. The more you take small steps toward your goals, the more your faith will grow.

Practical Steps to Cultivate Faith

1. **Visualize Your Goals Daily**: Spend five minutes every day visualizing your goals as though they've already been achieved. Picture every detail and feel the emotions of success—joy, pride, excitement. This will

help train your brain to focus on what's possible rather than what's holding you back.

2. **Detach from Certainty**: Remind yourself that certainty is a limitation. The greatest opportunities are found in the unknown. Journal about what living on the edge looks like for you and how you can embrace it.

3. **Reframe Fear**: Whenever fear arises, see it as a signal of growth, not failure. Remind yourself that fear is simply the edge of your comfort zone, and beyond that edge lies transformation.

4. **Take Small Leaps**: Build your faith by taking small, consistent actions that align with your vision. The more you prove to yourself that you can handle the unknown, the more confident and faithful you'll become.

5. **Gratitude for the Journey**: At the end of each day, reflect on what went well and express gratitude for even the smallest wins. Gratitude reinforces faith by reminding you of the progress you're making.

Faith is what allows you to live on the edge, to step into the unknown with courage and purpose. It's what separates those who stay in the safety of their comfort zones from those who create extraordinary lives. To live with faith is to trust that the edge isn't where you fall—it's where you soar

Why Mindset Matters Most

Mindset is not just a step; it's the foundation of the jump. Without it, every strategy, plan, and tool will fall short. Your mindset defines your reality, your ability to make decisions, and your resilience in the face of challenges. The beliefs you hold will either empower you or enslave you.

Faith, ownership, and the ability to lean into turbulence are not optional—they are essential. Together, they form the framework of the creator mindset. Faith allows you to trust in your vision, even when the path ahead is unclear. Ownership empowers you to take responsibility for your circumstances, your challenges, and your wins. And the ability to lean into turbulence ensures you're not only surviving the chaos but using it as a catalyst for growth.

When you shift your mindset, everything else follows. The people you attract into your life will change. Opportunities that align with your vision will appear. Challenges that once seemed insurmountable will become stepping-stones. Your entire perspective will shift from scarcity to abundance, from fear to possibility, from victim to creator.

But here's the truth: the transformation doesn't happen by chance. It requires a conscious decision to act. The moment you choose to reframe your challenges, rewrite your story, and step into the unknown, you set the stage for a life that reflects your vision instead of your fears.

Take a moment to imagine your life one year from now. What could you accomplish if you fully embraced this mindset? What would it feel like to live as the creator of your story rather than a passenger to your circumstances? The only thing standing between you and that life is the decision to shift. The time to make that choice is now.

Your life is waiting for you to step into it. Will you let fear or old beliefs hold you back, or will you make the shift and embrace the unknown? The choice is yours, and everything begins with that choice. Once you have made your decision, it is time to JUMP into action—with a plan, but the right kind of plan.

CHAPTER NINE

YOUR SAFETY NET IS A CAGE

WHEN I MADE THE DECISION TO LEAVE MY FIRM, I WASN'T JUST stepping into the unknown; I was stepping into my purpose. The exhilaration I felt wasn't about fearlessness but preparation. This wasn't just a dream; it was a calculated move toward the life I was meant to live.

There was a night when I stared at the ceiling, asking myself if I was making the biggest mistake of my life. The house was quiet. My wife was asleep. And I was lying there, calculating every scenario where this leap could go wrong. What if I failed? What if I let everyone down? What if I wasn't the leader I thought I was? It wasn't panic—it was stillness. A heavy kind of doubt that sat in my chest like a brick. But in that moment, I realized something: I wasn't scared because I was unprepared. I was scared because I cared. And that meant I was ready.

I didn't obsess over every challenge. I focused on what I could control. That became my compass.

We tell ourselves that having a "Plan B" is being responsible, but sometimes it's just a fear plan in disguise. I had to let go of the safety net and build something better.

That became my **Burn and Build Principle**: burn the boats of the past. Build the bridge forward—with intention.

The safety cage doesn't always look like a cage. It looks like logic. But if you're not careful, it becomes a prison built from your desire to avoid discomfort.

The Burn and Build Principle

We all like to believe we're building something new, but most of us are just trying to transition safely. We build the next chapter while holding tight to the last one. We want the leap, but with a safety net. We want the reward, but without the risk.

I've been there.

But at some point, I realized that if I was going to build something real, I had to stop asking the past to keep me safe.

I didn't just walk away; I burned the boats. And then I built the bridge forward.

Burning the boats meant letting go of the backup plan—the mental escape hatch I kept propped open in case I failed. And building the bridge meant doing the work: designing a vision, preparing the finances, and getting obsessed with execution.

This wasn't a reckless leap. It was a committed one.

And that's the difference.

People say, "Don't burn bridges." But when the bridge only leads back to a life that's killing your spirit, the brave thing is to torch it—and build a new one in the direction of your purpose.

Clarity wasn't just a feeling; it became a commitment. And commitment requires action. I treated this transition like training for a fight. I tracked every expense, cut the fluff, and prepared for the punches I couldn't see coming.

I wasn't just starting a business. I was building a runway to launch from, and that meant creating a business plan that could carry real weight. Not a pretty vision board, but a living document that turned my leap into measurable steps. Something I could follow when fear crept in, and the ground felt shaky.

Why a Business Plan Matters

A business plan is more than just an outline of your goals. It's a living, breathing document that:

- Keeps you focused on your mission: It defines your "why" and helps you stay aligned with your purpose.
- Identifies risks and solutions: It forces you to think critically about challenges and how to overcome them.
- Provides clarity for decision-making: It gives you a clear understanding of your finances, operations, and growth strategies.
- Builds confidence for lenders and partners: If you're seeking funding or forming partnerships, a solid business plan shows you're serious and prepared.

Reflection Prompt: Take a Moment to Think About Your Own Mission

Why are you pursuing this business? Write down your "why" in one sentence—it will serve as your anchor throughout this journey. Focus on what you can control.

The Essentials

When building a business, especially from scratch, there are countless factors that can feel overwhelming. The trick is to focus only on the things within your control and let go of everything else. Here are the major areas where your effort and preparation will pay off:

1. Finances and Credit

Your financial foundation is entirely within your control. Without proper planning and strong credit, your business may never get off the ground. Here's what to focus on:

- Master your credit: Understand how it works, improve your score, and prepare for applications strategically.
- Save aggressively: Build a cash buffer for unexpected challenges.

- Research funding options: Learn about loans, lines of credit, and refinancing.

When I refinanced my house, I knew exactly what my credit score would be before the lender pulled it. Why? Because I had researched the bureau they pulled from and the scoring model they used. That preparation wasn't just about securing the loan; it was about taking control of the process and eliminating the guesswork.

2. Legal Structures and Regulations

Your business structure impacts taxes, liability, and funding options. Take control by:

- Choosing the right structure: LLC, corporation, or partnership.
- Understanding industry-specific regulations, like ABS for law firms or management entities for med spas.
- Preparing for noncompete laws or licensing requirements.

As I mentioned earlier, in addition to owning my law firm, I also own a med spa business. I couldn't technically own the spa outright due to state laws. Instead, I owned the management entity that handles operations and revenue. This taught me to think creatively and research my options thoroughly.

3. The Initial Setup

Small decisions can have big impacts. Choose between virtual or physical based on your market and budget. (Tip: If a physical office feels overwhelming, consider starting with a virtual office or co-working space to minimize overhead.)

Invest in Tools That Streamline Operations and Improve Communication

I used to think technology was a nice-to-have. Something for the big firms with their fancy dashboards and six-figure software budgets. We were scrappy. We worked hard. We didn't need all that. Until one day, I woke up, looked at my overloaded team, my full caseload, my revenue … and realized:

We weren't running a business—we were surviving inside one. And here's the hard truth: **If your business runs on people alone, you don't own a business; you own a liability.**

Marketing and Branding

You can't control how people perceive your business, but you can control how you present it:

- **Branding:** Develop a story and identity that resonate with your audience.
- **Marketing:** Invest in what works—Google Ads, social media, SEO, or email marketing. Track your metrics and adjust your strategy as needed.

One of the biggest mindset shifts I had to make when I became an entrepreneur was rethinking what marketing really is.

For years, I believed that if I was good enough, people would find me. I prided myself on being a great lawyer—a workhorse. I thought keeping my head down and grinding would naturally generate business.

But the hard truth is, **the best product doesn't always win; the best story does.**

It took sitting at a Crisp conference for that reality to finally hit me. Speaker after speaker repeated the same message:

"If no one knows who you are, you can't help them—no matter how good you are."

That was my wake-up call.

Marketing Is a Mindset Shift

The first shift every entrepreneur must make is this:

Marketing isn't selling. It's connection. It's storytelling. It's serving others before serving yourself.

It's moving from a transactional mindset—*"How do I close this deal?"*—to a transformational one—*"How do I connect so deeply that people choose us because they trust us?"*

When I made that shift, marketing stopped feeling like self-promotion and started feeling like leadership.

StoryBrand: You're the Guide, Not the Hero

Donald Miller's *StoryBrand* framework drove this home for me:

- The client is the hero.
- You are the guide.

They're in the middle of their story, facing a problem. Your role is simple—show up with a plan and guide them toward success.

Yoda, not Luke. Mr. Miyagi, not Daniel-san.

Once you embrace that, you stop trying to be impressive—and start becoming *useful*.

How Story Changed Our Marketing—Mindset in Action

When we shifted our messaging from *"Here's how great we are"* to *"Here's how we help you,"* everything changed:

- Our ads stopped listing credentials and started speaking to the client's pain.

- Our videos focused on their fears and struggles, not our victories.
- Our messaging became simple and empathetic:
- *"Injured, overwhelmed, and don't know where to start? We'll guide you—every step of the way."*

That's the power of making your client the hero—they see themselves in your story.

Mindset Shift: *The goal isn't to be admired; it's to be trusted.*

Never Eat Alone: Marketing Is Connection

Where most business owners stop at storytelling, the best go deeper; they build relationships. That's the long game.

Keith Ferrazzi's book *Never Eat Alone* reinforced this truth: marketing is **every relationship you build**.

We stopped seeing marketing as ads or campaigns. Instead, we treated every meeting, every introduction, every check-in as marketing. Not because it would pay off tomorrow but because relationships compound over time:

- Grabbing coffee with referral partners
- Checking in with past clients—not to sell but to connect
- Attending community events and showing up consistently

The real shift came when I stopped asking, *"What can I get from this relationship?"* and started asking, *"How can I help?"*

The Law of Reciprocity: Lead with Value

Some of my best referral relationships weren't built by asking for cases; they were built because I genuinely looked for ways to help other attorneys.

- I introduced them to someone they could send a case to in a different state.
- I gave them access to data or insights that helped them grow their own practice.
- I shared what was working for us, not as a strategy but because I wanted to see them win, too.

That's when the relationship deepens—when people know you're not showing up with your hand out. You're showing up with **value**.

Mindset Shift: *Give first. Always.*

Hiring a Master Connector: Scaling the Relationship Mindset

Eventually, we realized the most valuable thing we could do wasn't just signing more cases; it was **scaling our generosity mindset.**

So, we hired the best in the business—someone whose zone of genius is building authentic, strategic relationships.

But here's the thing:

We didn't hire her because we had an opening. We hired her because she was the right person.

Our Master Connector didn't just step into the role; **she created it.** She's the visionary behind the **Rise Together Network**, a national alliance of vetted law firms committed to excellence, ethics, and collaboration. Her idea was to build a space where firms could connect, refer, and grow, all while keeping the client experience at the center.

We vet every firm in the network for:

- **Legal Competence** – Proven outcomes, litigation strength, and consistency.

- **Ethical Standards** – High integrity, clean records, and aligned values.
- **Client-Centric Culture** – Strong communication, compassion, and follow-through.
- **Operational Readiness** – Reliable systems, responsiveness, and execution.
- **Collaborative Mindset** – A willingness to support, share, and scale together.

But beyond the network, she embodies the essence of this role:

Her job isn't to close cases; it's to **open doors**.

To meet doctors, lawyers, and business leaders.

To build trust, follow up, and nurture relationships until we become the obvious answer to the question,

"Who can help me?"

This role doesn't pay off in transactions. It pays off in **trust**.

This position is **not easy to fill**—and that's exactly why it matters.

You're looking for someone who operates with **unshakable integrity** and who truly **embodies the brand** you've worked so hard to build.

When the right person walks in, you'll know.

And if you're lucky enough to find them, be ready.

Even if you weren't planning to hire, **you hire them anyway**. Because they'll change everything.

Mindset Shift: *Stop thinking marketing is paid ads. Start seeing it as paid relationships—cultivated with care.*

The Most Overlooked Marketing Channel: Your Intake Team

Here's where most businesses fail: they spend a fortune making the phone ring, then drop the ball the second someone picks up.

The truth is, **intake is marketing**. It's your first impression. Your brand's handshake. Your first—and sometimes last—chance to turn a stranger into a client.

We stopped seeing intake as a cost center and started treating it like the frontline of our brand. **That change in mindset was a game-changer.**

Here's how we operationalized it:

- **StoryBrand Scripts:** Every call starts with empathy: *"You've come to the right place. Our job is to guide you through this—every step of the way."*
- **Empathy Training:** Because no one hires a lawyer after being made to feel like a number.
- **AI Technology:** Real-time tools flag tone, empathy, and response speed—so we can coach in the moment.
- **Weekly Call Reviews:** Every lost call becomes a learning opportunity.
- **KPI and Incentives:** We reward empathy, connection, and speed, not just raw conversions.
- **Welcome Gifts:** Every new client gets a personal gift—because signing is the *beginning* of the relationship, not the end.

The Result?

We started hearing things like, *"You're the only firm that made me feel heard."* And when people feel safe with you, they hire you.

Your Action Plan: Build a Marketing Mindset Flywheel

If you do nothing else, do this: shift your marketing mindset. Here's how:

1. **Reframe your story:** Stop listing accomplishments. Start writing out your client's pain—and your role as their guide.
2. **Map your relationships:** Pick five past clients, five potential referral partners, and five people you admire.
3. Reach out—not to ask for but to offer help.
4. **Hire or become the Master Connector:** Dedicate time—or a full-time role—to building meaningful relationships.
5. **Audit your intake:** Does your intake team connect or just collect data? If it's the latter, fix it.
6. **Measure the right things:** Forget clicks. Track connection. Measure trust. Reward empathy.

One More Thing About Marketing
Marketing is a reflection of your mindset.
The best rainmakers don't chase clients; they attract them.
They don't sell; they guide.
They don't beg; they serve.
Marketing isn't a department; it's a way of showing up in the world.
Your job isn't to scream louder.
Your job is to make people feel seen, understood, and safe—so when the time comes, they choose you.
That's what it means to **become the rainmaker**.
And that's how you build a business that lasts.

Reflection Prompt:
Choosing How to Present Your Brand

Write down three qualities or values that you want your brand to communicate. How will these resonate with your target audience?

Technology is Leverage

The right technology doesn't replace your people; it **amplifies** them. It buys back your time, creates consistency, and gives you something every business needs to grow: **leverage**.

Every business runs on three currencies: **Time. Energy. Money.** And if you're not using technology, you're bleeding all three.

There was a time when every piece of our operation depended on a human memory:

- Need a case update? Call the paralegal and hope she's free.
- Want settlement numbers? Pray someone updated the Excel sheet.
- Client freaking out? Good luck finding the file.

We thought we were efficient.
We weren't.
We were running on muscle memory and burnout.

Technology Gives You Eyes on the Business

As we scaled, we realized something critical:
You can't lead what you can't see.
We used technology as our **eyes** into the firm. Because growth without visibility isn't growth—it's chaos. The right technology doesn't just organize your firm; it lets you *see* it.

- Are our paralegals and attorneys calling clients with updates? Just a click away.
- Are we getting demands out on time? Just a click away.
- How many lawsuits have we filed this month? Just a click away.

Technology gives you **real-time answers, not assumptions.**

It becomes your visibility system.

It becomes your **eyes as you scale.**

Because you can't rely on memory, meetings, or gut feelings when you're managing hundreds (or thousands) of files.

You need a **dashboard**, not a **guessing game.**

The Shift: From Surviving to Scaling

The truth is, we'd always had a case management system, but that wasn't enough.

It kept us organized, but it didn't give us **leverage**.

It didn't give us **insight**.

The real shift happened when we started layering technology that gave us **visibility, control, and predictability**, not just storage.

We implemented **EvenUp**, a software that helps us create polished demand packages, **summarizes medical records**, and provides real-time **case value analysis**. It saves our team hours and ensures consistency across every file.

We also integrated **Case Status**, a client communication platform that lets us track exactly how well our team is following up. It shows us—in real time—which clients are getting attention and which ones are overdue for an update.

That visibility allowed us to build systems around the **client experience**, proactively solving problems before they exploded and creating a smoother journey for every client.

Our attorneys are no longer buried in medical records; they're freed up to strategize, negotiate, and move cases forward faster.

Then, we layered in **Power BI**, a tool that allows us to track the numbers that matter: revenue per case, average cycle times, referral source ROI—in real time. For the first time, our data wasn't buried in spreadsheets; it was visual, accessible, and actionable.

And because knowing the numbers is one thing, but holding the team accountable is another, we added **Ninety.io**, a system that tracks goals, rocks, tasks, and to-dos for every team and every individual. It turned vague conversations into measurable progress.

For the first time, we weren't just working cases; **we were running a business built to scale.**

Building In-House Tools for the Future

And we didn't stop with off-the-shelf software.

We started **building our own technology**, not just to streamline but to evolve.

We built internal tools that allow us to get **text message updates directly from clients about their treatment**, so our team stays in the loop without constant outreach or manual notes.

We also developed **Grace**, our proprietary **voice AI**—a 24/7 backup for intake that never forgets a lead, never takes a break, and never drops the ball.

Grace isn't here to replace people; she's here to **reinforce** them. To support the human experience, not erase it.

Because we believe something simple but powerful:

If you want to survive and thrive in the future, you can't just think like a law firm—you have to think like a tech company.

The Excuses You're Telling Yourself

- "Tech is expensive."
  - — So are burnout, turnover, and missed opportunities.
- "My team doesn't like change."
  - — Neither did Blockbuster.

- "We're good at what we do; that should be enough."
  — It's not. Not anymore.

Where Technology Gives You the Edge

1. **Case Management and Automation**
   No more "Did we follow up?" moments. Triggers, deadlines, and reminders—built-in.
2. **Data-Driven Decisions**
   You stop guessing what's working; you know. Marketing ROI, case values, cycle times—all visible in real time.
3. **Client Experience**
   Automated updates and client portals create transparency. Faster communication = happier clients = more referrals.
4. **Freeing Up Your Team**
   They stop doing $10/hour admin work. They start doing $1,000/hour strategic work, the work that actually moves the needle.

To sum it up and give you ideas, here are, again, all the tools that freed up my team and me to do what matters most:

- **Case Management System (CMS)**: Keeps the entire operation organized and centralized.
- **EvenUp**: Summarizes medical records, helps generate demand packages, and delivers real-time value analysis.
- **Case Status**: Tracks client communication frequency and flags when follow-ups are overdue.
- **Power BI**: Visualizes key metrics: revenue per case, cycle times, marketing ROI, team productivity—all in real time.

- **Ninety.io**: Aligns the team with clear goals, rocks, and accountability, turning vague promises into measurable progress.
- **CRM and Automation Tools**: Automate follow-ups, send client updates, and reduce manual overhead.
- **Grace (Voice AI)**: Handles overflow and after-hours intake with consistency and professionalism.
- **A Client Text Update System**: Collects treatment progress directly from clients and integrates seamlessly into our team dashboards.

The Real Reason You're Hesitating

It's not about the cost.

It's about **control**.

Deep down, you're scared that if the business runs without you, you're not needed.

But here's the thing:

That's the goal.

You're not supposed to be needed every minute.

You're supposed to **build the machine**—not **be the machine**.

Your Action Step: Audit Where Tech Can Buy Back Your Time

Grab a notepad. Write down:

- What's repetitive?
- What's manual?
- What keeps falling through the cracks?

Chances are, there's tech that can solve it, and it's cheaper than you think.

Most leaders resist tech because it forces them to confront what's broken.

But the best entrepreneurs embrace it because they know technology doesn't replace the human touch … **it protects it.**

And when you build a business that runs with or without you?

That's freedom.

That's the goal.

The AI-Driven Leader: Let the Machine Work

The next evolution isn't just building a machine. It's building a *smart* one.

In the beginning, we didn't have KPIs.

We had hustle. We had heart. We had this belief that if we just worked harder—*longer hours, more cases, more people—*everything would fall into place.

So, when the firm expanded into workers' compensation, we went all in.

New team. New resources. Real money. Real time.

I didn't make the call to launch it—but I supported it.

I believed in the vision. I believed in the people.

And like anyone who's ever backed something with their full weight, I became emotionally attached.

So, even when the numbers didn't add up, I hesitated to shut it down. I wasn't clinging to the data—I was clinging to the emotional investment. .

The cases were moving, but the value wasn't there.

Still, I kept pushing. Kept justifying. Kept hoping.

Because walking away didn't feel strategic; it felt like failure.

Then I turned to the machine.

I ran the data—real case values, real costs, real cycle times, real impact on bandwidth.

AI didn't sugarcoat it. It didn't tell me what I wanted to hear.

It told the truth:

- Low net fees
- High resource drain
- Weak ROI relative to every other part of the business
- Massive opportunity cost

I wasn't shocked. But I was sobered.

It stripped away the emotional haze.

It gave me the clarity—and the permission—I needed to do what had to be done.

We shut it down.

And what followed was relief.

Because when you stop forcing what no longer fits, you create space for what does.

That one decision opened the door to a bigger question:

What else are we holding onto that the machine can now handle better than we can?

Since then, AI has become a second brain for the business. I've used it to:

- Forecast monthly collections based on real-time settlement modeling.
- Analyze financials to track where we're getting the highest return per employee hour.
- Prioritize leads based on projected lifetime value.
- Design operational systems and build KPIs from scratch.
- Trigger alerts when important metrics fall below thresholds.
- Eliminate entire categories of busywork—before they become drains on bandwidth.

We went from operating in the dark to leading in the light.

And we're just getting started.

Soon, AI will:

- Update clients automatically at key milestones.
- Request and follow up on medical records and bills.
- Reassign workloads based on real-time team capacity.
- Predict which cases are likely to fall apart *before* a human notices.

Right now, chasing medical records can eat up eight to ten hours per case over the course of a file.

With AI-triggered follow-ups and document automation, that could drop to thirty minutes.

This isn't about doing more.

It's about building smarter.

So you can do the things only a human can: build trust, cast vision, lead from the front.

Reflection Prompt: Finding Emotional Blind Spots

What are you still doing—or defending—out of emotional attachment, not evidence?

What would become possible if you let the data speak louder than your ego?

Mastering Credit: A Lesson in Control

One of the most empowering lessons I learned was mastering credit. At first, the topic felt overwhelming, but I quickly realized it was an area I could completely control with the right knowledge and preparation.

Here's what I focused on:

- Understanding Credit Scores: I researched the three bureaus and the scoring models that lenders use, from FICO to VantageScore. This allowed me to predict my score and prepare for credit applications.

- Timing Credit Applications: I learned when accounts reported to the bureaus and ensured my credit profile was in the best shape before applying for loans.
- Securing Loans: I explored collateral-backed loans and understood how to position my assets strategically.

When I first started researching credit, I was intimidated by all the jargon—FICO scores, credit utilization, inquiries—but I broke it down piece by piece. Every small improvement I made gave me a sense of control over something I'd previously ignored. By the time I applied for a loan, I knew exactly how my profile would look to the lender, and that confidence was invaluable.

Building the Business Plan

All this preparation culminated in my business plan—a roadmap that turned my vision into actionable steps. Here's how I controlled each part of the process:

1. Executive Summary
A high-level overview of your mission, goals, and business model.

2. Financial Plan
Your financial blueprint, including:

- Cash Flow Statement: To track money moving in and out of your business.
- Profit and Loss Statement (P&L): To measure revenue, expenses, and profitability. That's when I realized revenue is just noise if profit isn't built in from day one. Profit isn't an event. It's a discipline. And like any discipline, it changes your behavior—if you let it.

What the book *Profit First* taught me—and what most business owners miss—is that profit isn't something you *hope* shows up at the end of the month. It's a habit. A muscle. A way of running your business that forces better decisions every single day. Because once you start pulling profit off the top—every time money hits your account—everything shifts. You stop making bloated hires just because you're "busy." You stop taking every client just because they have a checkbook. You stop chasing revenue because, without profit, it's noise.

- Break-Even Analysis: To calculate how much revenue you need to cover costs.

My partner was the first to read Profit First, and I'll be honest—I didn't jump on it right away. At the time, I thought I had a decent handle on the numbers. But the more we talked, the more I realized we were still flying blind.

Eventually, I picked it up. And I'm glad I did. We started implementing the system that same quarter, allocating revenue into separate accounts for profit, taxes, owner's pay, and operating expenses. It forced us to get brutally honest about how sustainable our business model really was.

The biggest shift? It wasn't just financial; it was mental. We stopped hiring out of panic. We stopped justifying bloated expenses. We stopped chasing growth without discipline. Profit First became more than a cash management tool; it became the habit that trained us to think like true business owners.

But discipline isn't just about cutting; sometimes **adding** people increases profit.

Many business owners, especially after going through tough times, get scared to hire.

They stall. They sit on their cash. They convince themselves they're being smart when really, they're just stuck.

The truth? **Staying small is just as risky as growing too fast.**

In both my businesses, some of the most profitable moves we made were hiring the *right* people at the *right* time.

Bringing in a **nurse practitioner** or **another attorney** wasn't just an expense; it was an investment that created revenue.

But you have to know the math:

What does this person cost, and what's the projected revenue they generate once fully ramped?

That's the KPI test—and it keeps you honest.

The Real Danger: Empty Seats with No Plan to Fill Them

Businesses bleed cash when they hire talent but fail to get them to capacity fast enough.

You can't just hire and hope. You need a plan.

For example:

- A nurse practitioner might be able to see ten patients a day. Do you hire when you're one patient over capacity? Five? Ten?
- A lawyer might manage forty cases. When do you bring them on, and how fast do you fill their caseload?

Creative Ways to Shorten the Ramp to Capacity

Here's where disciplined businesses separate from average ones—they attack the ramp-up period:

- **Pre-sell services** tied to the new hire.
- **Run promotions** to drive traffic straight to the new team member.
- **Leverage referral partners** to send overflow business to fill capacity fast.
- **Redistribute low-value work** to free up top producers and give new hires immediate wins.

- **Incentivize production**—align bonuses with filling their book quickly.
- **Launch targeted campaigns** designed to fill *their* schedule, not just general leads.

Debt Versus No Debt—Both Can Be Right If You're Disciplined

And this is where the debt conversation becomes real.

Do you wait until cash flow allows? Or do you borrow to move faster?

Both approaches work—if you're disciplined.

On one side, you've got the **conservative approach**:

No debt, no loans. Grow slowly. Earn your expansion.

On the other side, you've got the **Robert Kiyosaki model**:

Smart debt is leverage. Use other people's money to grow faster—if you're buying cash flow, not liabilities.

And the truth? **Both are right.**

Debt amplifies whatever system you've built.

- If your model is broken, debt buries you faster.
- If your model is tight, debt is rocket fuel.

The real question is: **What is this debt buying you?**

- Covering payroll? Dangerous.
- Funding a revenue-producing hire with a clear path to ROI? Smart.

The Discipline Is the Reward—Just Like Training for a Marathon

Here's the thing about discipline—it's not a one-time decision. It's a practice.

Profit isn't something you *hope* for; it's something you train for, just like running a marathon.

You don't show up on race day and expect to finish if you haven't put in the miles.

You build the habit. You track your pace. You show up, even when it's hard—especially when it's hard.

Business is the same way.

You don't get profitable once and stay there by accident.

You get there by consistently making disciplined decisions, over and over again.

You know your numbers.

You check your KPIs.

You hire when it's smart.

You protect your profit—because it protects everything else.

And here's the truth:

The more consistent you are, the easier it gets.

You stop feeling like you're sprinting just to survive—and start running your race with confidence, knowing exactly where you're going.

Because that's what this really is—**your race**.

No one's coming to save you.

No one's going to build your dream but you.

Profit is how you stay in the game long enough to win it.

You don't go out of business because you're not profitable.

You go out of business because you run out of cash.

I wish someone had screamed that in my face when I started.

We were growing fast. Revenue was pouring in on paper. I had a team. We were marketing hard, signing cases, opening new ventures. From the outside, it looked like we were crushing it.

Then came payroll week.

I looked at the account and thought, *There's no way this number is right.*

But it was.

That's when I learned: profit is theory. Cash is reality.

Revenue Feels Good—Cash Pays the Bills.

You can be signing cases or clients left and right, but if money isn't actually hitting your account—or if your overhead is running laps around your collections—you're in trouble.

I had to learn this the hard way.

And I had to learn it in two different businesses.

My law firm is an accounts receivable (AR) business. We do the work upfront, often over the course of months or years, and then wait for the money to arrive after settlement.

My med spa is a paid-up-front business. Patients pay before we provide the service, giving us money in the bank before the expenses hit.

Both have their challenges.

But one thing is consistent: cash flow is king.

Are You AR or Paid Up Front? Know the Game You're Playing

The following outlines both types to help you determine what your business will be:

Accounts Receivable (AR) Business – Law Firm

- You do the work first, often for months or years.
- You wait for the result—then the check.
- Meanwhile, you're covering salaries, rent, software, vendors, and case costs.

If you're not tracking your cash, this model will bury you.

Paid Up Front – Med Spa

- You get paid before the service.
- Cash flow is more predictable—but only if you're watching your burn rate and delivering value.

Both models can work. But only if you know how the money moves.

I've Made Every Cash Flow Mistake You Can Imagine

- Hiring too fast because revenue "felt good"
- Spending emotionally instead of strategically
- Letting accounts receivable stack up without a follow-up process
- Running marketing campaigns without tracking ROI
- Thinking "profit" in QuickBooks meant I was fine

I confused growth with health.

I learned that scaling without watching cash is like adding passengers to a boat with a leak.

The Turning Point: Build a 14-Week Cash Flow Forecast

I started treating cash like oxygen.

We built a simple spreadsheet:

- What's coming in this week?
- What's going out?
- What's our projected balance?

No fluff. No fancy software. Just visibility.

We reviewed it every week. It became our rhythm.

And once I started watching the money before it left the account, I realized something:

Cash doesn't lie.

A Blind Spot That Hit My Bottom Line

At our med spa, we were seeing patients, billing insurance, and operating under the assumption that everything was running smoothly.

Then one day, I found out we'd been out of contract with a major insurance provider—and hadn't known for a long time.

We never received a formal notice. We weren't tracking expiration dates.

We didn't even have a system in place to monitor our contracts.

That one blind spot cost us a substantial amount of money.

But more importantly, it cracked something open for me:

It wasn't just a billing error. It was a leadership lesson.

You Don't Find Blind Spots by Guessing

There are two ways to find blind spots:

1. You fall into a hole.
2. You ask someone who's already looking at it.

After that incident, I went straight to my team and asked:

- What's working?
- What's not?
- What blind spots are we not seeing?

Here's the truth:

Don't expect to like the answers you get.

But if you want to grow, you have to hear them anyway.

As your company grows, this may mean skipping over middle management and speaking directly to the people doing the work. Not because your managers aren't capable but because the rawest insight lives at the edges of your business.

You'll be shocked at what people see—if you give them the space to tell you.

Lesson: Fixing the System Is Worth the Hit

After that financial hit, we built out a full contract tracking system—automated reminders, a renewal schedule, clear ownership. But the bigger win was learning to regularly ask:

Where else are we operating on assumptions instead of clarity?

Now, we perform skills and systems audits on a regular basis—not just to plug holes but to get ahead of them.

Because cash doesn't just leak through invoices; it leaks through assumptions.

What I Wish I Knew Sooner

1. Cash > Profit

   You can be profitable and broke if receivables don't convert to deposits.

2. Track AR like your life depends on it—because it does.

   Assign someone to follow up. Make it part of your culture.

3. Have two to three months of runway saved.

   Not for growth—for survival. Your peace of mind is worth it.

4. Delay costs. Accelerate cash.

   Negotiate payment terms. Ask for deposits. Create incentives for early payment.

5. Revenue is a vanity metric.

   Cash flow is your lifeline. Profit is a goal. Cash is the game.

Reflection Prompt: Know Your Cycle

Grab a whiteboard or a notepad and answer:

- Do you get paid before, during, or after service?
- How long does it take from signing a client to getting paid?
- Where are you leaking cash right now?
- What can you cut, renegotiate, or automate?

Cash Doesn't Lie

Cash doesn't care how passionate you are.

It doesn't care how big your vision is.

It doesn't care how many hours you're putting in.

It just asks: Can you survive the month?

Get honest with your numbers. Not someday. Not later. Now.

Because when you master your cash, you don't just survive; you gain the power to build.

And that's the real freedom behind the JUMP.

Predictable Cash Flow Starts with Paying Attention

Most business owners treat cash flow like a mystery.

They're surprised when the bank account dips.

They're shocked when it runs dry.

They call it unpredictable, but that's not true.

Cash flow isn't unpredictable. It's just untracked.

In most businesses, the patterns are right in front of you. You just have to stop guessing and start watching.

Contingency-Based Businesses (Like PI Firms)

If you're running a personal injury firm, you're in an accounts receivable business with a built-in delay, but that delay is actually predictable.

Here's how it typically works:

1. The case settles.
2. You wait for the check.
3. You finalize reductions.
4. You wait for the check to clear trust.
5. You pay the client and collect your fee.

From the outside, this looks like chaos. But once you know your numbers, it becomes trackable:

- What's your average time from settlement to cleared trust account funds?
- What percentage of cases close within thirty, sixty, or ninety days of settlement?
- What's your average monthly case volume?
- What percentage of your pipeline is currently in the "settled, not closed" stage?

When you answer those questions, you stop relying on instinct—and you start building a forecast.

You can spot cash flow crunches coming weeks in advance.

Retail and Scheduled Service Businesses (Like Med Spas)

In businesses like med spas, you're dealing with up-front cash, which makes forecasting easier in some ways—but still vulnerable if you don't watch the details.

Here's how to start predicting:

Look at your appointment book for the next thirty to sixty days.

- Track your average cancellation rate.
- Measure your average ticket size.
- Consider promotional periods, membership renewals, or retail cycles.

This gives you a rough forecast of revenue. But don't stop there. Ask:

- When are your busiest months?

- What products or services spike during those periods?
- What events (holidays, back-to-school, new year) shift client behavior?

Understand Seasonality or Be Surprised by It

Every business has seasonal tendencies, even if they're subtle. The only difference is whether you're paying attention. For example:

- Personal injury firms often collect more toward the end of the year because insurance companies are motivated to get cases off the books before closing theirs.
- Med spas might peak in different seasons depending on geography. In some places, summer is peak body season. In others, it's slow because everyone is traveling.

You don't need to guess. You need to ask:

- What did last year look like by month?
- Are there predictable dips or spikes?
- Have I budgeted for the valleys?
- Do I staff and market according to the seasons, or do I operate the same year-round?

Your Forecast Doesn't Need to Be Perfect—Just Directional

This isn't about building a Wall Street model. It's about clarity. When you know how your cash actually behaves, you can:

- Decide when to invest and when to hold.
- Hire with confidence—or delay strategically.
- Prepare your team for leaner months (instead of pretending they aren't coming).

Ask yourself right now:

- *Do I know my average delay between work done and cash received?*
- *Do I track pipeline volume by stage?*
- *Do I know my busy versus slow seasons by revenue—not just gut feel?*
- *Do I watch the calendar the same way I watch the bank account?*

If the answer is no, that's not a failure. That's a starting point.

Don't Just Watch the Numbers—Study Them

Forecasting isn't just for CFOs.

It's for leaders who want to build with confidence.

If you want predictable cash, start by predicting patterns.

Because in almost every business, they're already there, waiting to be noticed.

If finances aren't your strong suit, invest in bookkeeping software or hire an accountant early on. It's a small cost that can save you from major headaches later.

Marketing and Sales Strategy

How you'll attract and retain clients:

- Branding strategies to build trust and recognition
- A mix of advertising (Google Ads, SEO, social media)
- A clear sales funnel, from lead generation to conversion

Even with all this preparation, the leap was still terrifying. But I knew my parachute was packed. I had done everything in my power to prepare. I focused on what I could control—my finances, my plan, and my mindset—and began to embrace what I couldn't.

When the time came to jump, I didn't hesitate. The fear didn't disappear, but it transformed into something else: momentum. I wasn't just starting a business; I was stepping into my purpose. And as I took the leap, I knew one thing for sure: I was ready for whatever came next.

The key mindset for your JUMP is focusing on what's within your control. You can't predict every challenge or eliminate every risk, but you can prepare, plan, and act with intention.

When you focus on what you can control, you stop wasting energy on the "what ifs" and start building a foundation for success. Your business plan isn't just a document; it's your compass. It turns uncertainty into opportunity and vision into action. And when you take the leap, your business plan isn't just a tool; it's a compass. A decision to trust yourself. A commitment to clarity.

Because once you build that bridge forward, you don't need the cage anymore.

You don't need the safety net that kept you small, the logic that kept you waiting, or the backup plan that was never really meant to catch you; it was meant to keep you still.

The truth is, the cage was never locked.

You were just taught to fear the door.

But freedom was always on the other side, and the key was in your hand

You're not here to stay safe.

You're here to soar.

Burn the boats.

Build the bridge.

Then, walk across it—toward the life you were meant to live.

Reflection Prompt: What's Your Safety Net?

What safety net are you still clinging to—just in case?

Where are you asking the past to protect you from a future you've already outgrown?

Write down:

- One belief you're ready to release.
- One fear you're ready to walk toward.
- One action you can take this week to build your bridge forward.

You've taken the leap.

You've built your runway.

Now comes the part most people skip—the *deep commitment to your identity as a leader.*

In the next chapter, we'll explore what happens **after** the JUMP—when you realize you're not just running a business …

You're building a legacy.

Let the boats burn. Build the bridge forward. And when fear returns, remember: you're not falling—you're flying.

CHAPTER TEN

WHO'S REALLY RUNNING YOUR LIFE?

Taking the jump means there's no turning back. It's not a half-hearted decision or one made with escape routes in mind. The only way to succeed in entrepreneurship is to commit fully to burning the boats and removing the option of retreat. When you go all in, the stakes become real, and with that comes the energy and focus necessary to succeed.

Steven Pressfield, in *The War of Art*, describes resistance as a force that rises when we're on the verge of something meaningful. The fear, doubt, and hesitation you feel are indicators that you're standing at the edge of your growth. The only way forward is through.

Burning the Boats

The concept of "burning the boats" comes from a famous historical story attributed to Hernán Cortés. When Cortés and his men landed on the shores of Mexico in 1519, he ordered his crew to burn their ships, eliminating any possibility of retreat. His message was clear: they had no choice but to move forward, fight, and succeed because there was no way to go back.

This idea is a powerful metaphor for commitment. To "burn the boats" means to eliminate any safety net or fallback option that might tempt you to retreat when things get tough. It's about removing the possibility of giving up and forcing yourself to focus entirely on the path ahead.

Why "Burning the Boats" Matters in Entrepreneurship

1. **Forces Total Commitment**
   When you have no way to retreat, you become fully present and focused because failure is not an option. This level of commitment unlocks creativity, persistence, and resourcefulness you may not realize you have.

2. **Eliminates Distraction and Doubt**
   When you keep a safety net, even subconsciously, you divide your energy. Part of you will always consider retreat as an option, making it easier to hesitate or give less than 100 percent. Burning the boats removes the mental clutter, allowing you to channel all your energy into building your new path.

3. **Builds Trust in Yourself**
   When you go all in, you send a message to yourself and others: "I believe in this vision." That belief is magnetic. It inspires your team, attracts opportunities, and strengthens your own confidence. Burning the boats forces you to bet on yourself and take ownership of your destiny.

For years, I had been grappling with the tension between what I wanted to create and the safety of the role I had built at my firm. My turning point came when I sought investment from my boss to build something I truly believed in. He refused.

At first, I felt a mix of anger and devastation. His refusal felt like a dismissal of my potential. But deep down, I knew that this was the moment. If I didn't leave then, I never would.

I was terrified. What if I failed? What if I couldn't provide for my family? These thoughts kept me awake at night, playing out worst-case scenarios in vivid detail. But alongside the fear was something else: excitement. For the first time, I wasn't just imagining what life could look like if I pursued my dreams; I was actively choosing to chase them. The mix of fear and excitement propelled me forward.

Shortly after leaving, my father passed away. His death became a profound reminder of what it means to let go of the past. My dad had taught me countless lessons in life—about strength, perseverance, and love, but ironically, the biggest lesson came in his death.

My dad had always been a fighter, someone who defied odds and clung to life with an unmatched passion. But even the strongest among us must eventually surrender. Watching him in those final moments, I understood that letting go isn't about weakness; it's about faith—faith in what lies ahead, faith in the unknown, and faith that letting go of what no longer serves you clears the way for something beautiful to emerge.

Leaving my firm was my own act of surrender. I had poured so much of myself into building that operation, but it no longer aligned with who I was or where I wanted to go. My dad's passing taught me that to embrace the future, you have to release the past. In doing so, I was able to create something much more powerful: a firm built on my why and a life rooted in purpose.

Fear as a Guide and Failure as Growth: A Unified Perspective on Transformation

Fear is often misinterpreted as a warning to stop, but it's actually a guide pointing toward what truly matters. Steven Pressfield, in *The War of Art*, describes resistance as an internal force that arises whenever we're on the brink of meaningful change. The more resistance we feel, the more significant the opportunity for growth.

When fear shows up, it's not a signal to retreat—it's an invitation to lean in. Resistance indicates that you're stepping into the unknown, a space where transformation takes place.

Leaving my stable job to start something from scratch was one of the most terrifying decisions of my life. The weight of uncertainty and the fear of failure loomed large, making me question if I was ready for such a leap. But I learned to see fear as fuel.

Every time I felt the urge to retreat, I reminded myself of my "why." I leaned into the JUMP Method—justifying my why, uncovering limiting beliefs, and shifting my mindset. With every small step, I reframed fear as evidence that I was on the right path, embracing it as a sign of progress rather than a roadblock.

Failure Doesn't Exist: It's All Growth

What many perceive as failure is simply part of the process, a stepping-stone on the path to success. The idea of failure as a definitive endpoint is a myth. In reality, failure is a *growth trial*—a necessary stage that teaches, refines, and strengthens. The only true failure is quitting, and when your "why" is strong enough, quitting isn't an option. There are two things failure can teach us:

1. Failure is a stepping-stone, not a dead end.
2. What you don't know is an opportunity to grow.

Personal Growth Trials

My entrepreneurial journey has been shaped by a similar mindset. In the early days of marketing my firm, I anticipated that some campaigns would fail. And they did—sometimes spectacularly. Instead of fearing failure, I embraced it as feedback, using each setback to refine my approach.

One of my early marketing campaigns flopped because I

underestimated the investment required to reach niche markets. Instead of seeing this as a failure, I analyzed why it didn't work and adjusted my strategy. Over time, I discovered the thresholds needed to make certain channels effective. These lessons lowered my case acquisition costs and became the foundation of my scaling strategy.

Embracing Fear and Failure as Catalysts

When you reframe fear as a compass and failure as growth, both become powerful tools for transformation. Here's how to adopt this mindset:

1. **Use Fear as a Guide**
   Lean into resistance. When fear arises, recognize it as a sign that you're stepping into uncharted, transformative territory.

2. **Reframe Failure as Feedback**
   Each setback offers valuable lessons. Instead of focusing on what went wrong, use the insights to improve and innovate.

3. **Expect Growth Trials**
   Understand that the path to success involves trial and error. Some efforts will fail, but every attempt moves you closer to your goals.

4. **Focus on the Wins**
   Don't dwell on missteps. Analyze them, extract the lessons, and pour your energy into what works.

5. **Play the Long Game**
   Success is a cumulative process. Each growth trial lays the foundation for greater achievements.

Fear Fuels Progress; Failure Fuels Resilience

Transformation happens at the intersection of fear and failure. Fear pushes you into the unknown, while failure provides the lessons needed to navigate it. Growth isn't linear; it's a series of cycles involving risk, missteps, and refinement.

When you embrace fear and failure, they become your greatest allies, guiding you toward your vision and arming you with the resilience to achieve it.

Reframe Failure as Growth

Entrepreneurship means embracing failure as part of the process. As Jocko Willink writes in *Extreme Ownership*, you have to take radical responsibility for your outcomes—good or bad. Every failure is a lesson, a step toward mastery. Commit to learning, and you'll never truly fail. And sometimes, that means learning to embrace knowing what you don't know.

Success in business isn't about knowing or doing everything yourself. Trying to do so would be a disservice to both your business and yourself. It would mean abandoning your zone of genius—the unique gifts and abilities that only you bring to the table.

Stepping into fear doesn't mean jumping without a parachute. It means embracing the truth of who you are: a person with both gifts and limitations. Your limitations aren't flaws to be fixed; they are part of the intricate design that makes you *you*. They are beautiful because they create the space for others to step in, contribute, and thrive.

Early on, you will be forced to handle things that don't perfectly align with your strengths. You might have to manage marketing, handle bookkeeping, or oversee operations. The chaos of juggling these responsibilities is almost inevitable when resources are tight. But as you push through, your goal isn't to master everything; it's to identify what truly energizes you and what doesn't.

As your business grows and revenue starts to build, you'll have the opportunity to offload the tasks that pull you out of alignment. This isn't about avoiding responsibility; it's about doing what you do best and allowing others to do the same. You'll quickly learn that the things you dislike doing—or simply aren't skilled at—are often the very things that others excel at and find immense joy in.

Recognizing what you don't know and delegating those responsibilities isn't a weakness; it's an act of leadership. It creates space for others to thrive and allows you to focus your energy on the areas where you can have the greatest impact.

Assessing Your Gaps and Building Your Team

To go all in, you need a team that complements your strengths. Follow this process to identify your skill gaps and create a hiring or delegation plan:

1. **Identify Your Unique Abilities**
   - What are you naturally great at? What energizes you?
   - Use tools like *StrengthsFinder 2.0* to clarify your strengths.

2. **Recognize Your Weaknesses**
   - Where do you struggle or procrastinate?
   - Be honest about what you don't enjoy or aren't skilled at.

3. **Hire the Right People**
   - Build a team of specialists who excel in your weak areas.
   - Listen to Jim Collins' advice in the book Good to Great: "Get the right people on the bus."

4. **Delegate Effectively**
   - Let go of tasks that don't align with your strengths.

Trust your team to deliver, and focus your energy where it has the greatest impact. But here's the truth nobody says out loud:

Delegation too early, especially expensive delegation, can crush your cash flow.

You hire a high-level assistant, a manager, or a director because you're overwhelmed and "ready to scale." But if the work they're doing doesn't free you up to do something more valuable, or if their output doesn't generate ROI quickly, you've just added overhead with no leverage.

You didn't delegate.

You increased your burn rate.

Delegate Low-Value Tasks First and Earn the Right to Let Go

This is why I coach entrepreneurs to buy back their time in layers.

1. Start with $10/hour tasks: Admin work, scheduling, data entry, routine follow-ups
2. Graduate to $100/hour tasks: Customer service, intake, invoicing, basic marketing
3. Eventually delegate $1,000/hour tasks: Management, strategy, leadership, decision-making

If you skip straight to the $1,000/hour tier before your business can support it, you're not scaling—you're sinking.

When I Delegated Too Early—And Had to Take It All Back

Early on, I delegated case handling so I could focus on building the firm. It seemed like the right move: get out of the weeds and into the vision.

But we were growing fast, too fast.

Revenue on paper looked great, but cash flow couldn't keep up.

Eventually, I had to step back in. Not because I wanted to but because we simply couldn't afford that delegation yet.

That moment taught me this:

Delegation must be driven by two things: putting people in their zone of genius and

making sure the business can financially support it.

It's not just about leadership. It's about discipline.

And that ties directly back to what I teach with the concept of Cash Doesn't Lie.

The Inner Battle of Letting Go

Even after I said I wanted to delegate, my brain was still looking for reasons to prove it was a mistake.

I'd check their work.

Not to support but to catch them slipping.

If something wasn't done exactly the way I would've done it, even if the result was still solid, I'd get annoyed. I'd tell myself it wasn't working. I'd find every excuse to jump back in.

Truth is, I wasn't ready to let go.

And I wasn't judging their performance; I was defending my belief that I was still the only one who could do it right.

It was perfectionism disguised as leadership.

Control disguised as care.

That's when I heard Dan Martell say something that changed everything:

"Eighty percent done by someone else is better than 100 percent done by you."

At first, I resisted it. But then I realized that if I hold out for perfection, I'll always be the bottleneck. I'll never let people grow. I'll never create real leverage. Leadership isn't doing it all perfectly. It's empowering others to grow while freeing yourself to focus on what only you can do.

Now I ask three questions before handing anything off:

4. Do I understand this well enough to explain it simply?
5. Do I have the right person, with the right wiring, for this task?
6. Is there a system or feedback loop in place to track progress?

If the answer to any of those is no, I'm not ready to delegate it, and neither is the business.

Delegating what you're bad at or hate doing? That's easy.

The real test comes when you have to pick up something you're good at but no longer love.

When the business demands it.

When the team isn't ready yet.

When the money just isn't there to outsource it.

There will be seasons in the journey where you have to step into roles you've outgrown, not forever but for the sake of the mission.

That's not failure.

That's leadership.

This Is Temporary, But It's Necessary

The goal isn't to stay in that role forever; it's to meet the moment with discipline instead of resentment. Because what you're doing is buying time and space for your team to grow, for the revenue to catch up, for the business to stabilize. And when you do that with the right mindset, not as a martyr but as a builder, you'll come out the other side stronger, clearer, and better equipped to fully step into your genius.

The mindset shift is this:

You're not stuck; you're being sharpened.

You're not backsliding; you're bridging the gap.

You're not failing; you're finishing the foundation.

Yes, delegation is freedom.

Yes, your zone of genius matters.

But you're building something bigger than comfort.

And when the time is right?

You delegate it.

You elevate.

You expand.

But until then, you show up, lead with intention, and hold the line. Because that's what real builders do.

The All-In Mindset

Brené Brown reminds us that vulnerability is not weakness; it's courage in action. Going all in means exposing yourself to uncertainty and risk, but it also opens the door to connection and opportunity. Trust yourself and trust the process.

The Dip and the Breakthrough

Seth Godin explains that every worthwhile endeavor includes a "dip"—a period of struggle where quitting feels easier than pressing forward. This is where most people give up. But if you can endure the dip, you'll emerge stronger and more prepared for the success that lies on the other side.

Embracing Uncertainty

There were moments when I almost retreated to the safety of a nine-to-five job. When uncertainty pressed hard, I returned to JUMP—Why, Beliefs, Mindset—and recommitted. Each step forward reinforced the leap.

As the business grew, so did my confidence. Delegating tasks to my team allowed me to focus on growth and strategy. I stopped trying to do it all and started doing what I was meant to do. The results were undeniable.

How to Plan Your All-In Strategy

1. **Fear Mapping**
   - Write down your biggest fears about taking the jump.
   - For each fear, identify the worst-case scenario and how you would handle it.
   - Reframe each fear as an opportunity for growth.

1. **Gap Assessment**
   - List your strengths and weaknesses.
   - Identify the tasks you should delegate.
   - Create a hiring plan to fill your gaps.

2. The Commitment Contract
   You don't need another plan—you need a promise. This is that moment. Write a one-page letter to yourself that serves as your **Commitment Contract.** This isn't a worksheet or a journal prompt. This is a declaration.
   - Declare your jump.
   - Justify your why.
   - Define the vision.
   - Name the cost of not following through.

Sign it. Date it. Frame it.

This contract isn't for your boss. It's not for your friends. It's for you, and your future self is going to read it one day and either thank you or remind you that you broke a promise.

Burn the boats. Write the contract. Then build the bridge. Commitment isn't always spoken, but you feel it. You're no longer flirting with leaving. You've left internally, and the world just hasn't caught up.

You've committed.

And that's what confused the people around me, especially my boss.

Why would someone walk away from a generous compensation package, a growing client base, and a clear path to earn lot of money?

The answer:

Because once you commit at that level, external logic can't justify staying where your soul doesn't belong.

I was already making really good money—and I had just started hitting my stride. Referrals were picking up. My name was circulating. People didn't just trust my results—they trusted me. And that trust was compounding.

I was building success inside someone else's vision.

But I wasn't chasing money; I was chasing meaning.

And when it came time to leap, I didn't do it blindly. I had side businesses generating income, a real estate portfolio, and a strong savings cushion.

And I cashed it all in.

When I put in my notice, my boss looked at me like I'd lost my mind.

Maybe I had.

He immediately called for an exit interview, and the first thing he said was:

"You make good money."

But that was the problem.

What I wanted couldn't be measured in compensation. I wanted freedom and alignment with my vision. I was done building someone else's dream while ignoring the pull toward my own.

It scared my parents. And that was okay.

Their fear wasn't mine to carry—and they carried it because they loved me.

They believed in safety, in stability, in not risking what you've worked so hard to build. But I believed in something else: that sometimes, the safest thing you can do for your soul is leap.

I took every asset I had built over the years and poured it into the one thing that didn't yet exist—my own firm. My own name. My own vision.

And I took the rest of it … and put it into a med spa.

Two bets, same reason: I was ready to stop surviving and start creating.

The early days were brutal. I was spending aggressively on advertising, laying down infrastructure, and investing in people. I told myself I wouldn't take a paycheck the first year—and I didn't. But the mental toll was heavier than I expected.

Watching the money go out while the returns trickled in was a daily test of faith. There were nights I stared at the ceiling, my chest tight, wondering if I'd made a mistake, if I'd overestimated myself, if I'd lose it all.

I questioned my timing, my strategy, even my sanity. But not the decision.

There is no looking back.

And moving forward? It was the scariest thing I've ever done. But I did it anyway.

Because something inside me had already decided: this wasn't just a career move—it was a commitment to myself.

That was my Commitment Contract. Silent, but irreversible.

Once I made it, it started making me.

I stopped trying to make the leap "safely." I stopped looking for a net.

The moment I chose to build my own future, I started becoming the person who could.

That's the paradox no one talks about. You don't become "ready" and then jump.

You jump—and then you become ready

That commitment didn't just change how I thought; it changed what I was willing to burn.

Because once you've decided to bet on yourself, you realize something hard but necessary:

You can't build something great while holding onto something safe.

A piece of your identity has to burn so your purpose can breathe.

And so, I burned.

Old titles. Old systems. Old habits.

What came next wasn't just about building a firm; it was about rebuilding myself.

Burn the Boats, Build the Bridge

Going all in isn't easy. It's messy, scary, and unpredictable. But it's also the only way to achieve something extraordinary. When you commit fully—without hesitation or retreat—you unlock a level of focus and determination you didn't know you had.

The jump isn't just a leap into the unknown; it's a declaration of belief in yourself and your vision. Burn the boats behind you, start building the bridge to your future, and know your worth.

I call this the Burn and Build Principle—a balance between relentless commitment and disciplined preparation. One eliminates distraction; the other prevents destruction.

Reflection Prompt: Burn to Build

What do you need to burn—and what must you now build?

CHAPTER ELEVEN

NO ONE MAKES THE JUMP ALONE: THE IMPORTANCE OF MENTORSHIP

MAKING THE LEAP INTO ENTREPRENEURSHIP CAN FEEL OVERwhelming. It's like standing on the edge of a cliff, staring into the unknown. In those moments, it's easy to believe you have to *earn* your place—that you're not ready, not smart enough, not worthy of success yet. Your worth isn't something you need to prove. It's something you already carry.

And here's a secret: no one makes the jump alone. Behind every successful entrepreneur is a team of mentors, coaches, and accountability partners who guided them, supported them, and pushed them to take bold actions. This chapter is about finding those people and building the network that will turn your leap into a calculated, successful move.

Mentors don't give you worth; they help you unlock what's already there.

Types of Mentors to Seek Out

Not all mentors are created equal. Depending on where you are in your journey, you'll need different kinds of guidance. Here's a breakdown of the four types of mentors to consider and what each can offer:

1. Industry Expert Mentor
   - What They Offer: Specific knowledge and insights into the industry you want to break into.

- Why They're Important: They've been where you want to go. They know the common pitfalls, the shortcuts, and the unspoken rules of the game.
- How to Find Them: Attend industry events, network on LinkedIn, or look for established professionals willing to share their expertise.

When I started my firm, I didn't know the intricacies of running a personal injury practice. I sought out a mentor who had scaled their practice and understood the dynamics of the industry. Their insights helped me avoid costly mistakes, like overspending on the wrong marketing channels, and pushed me to invest in strategies that worked.

2. Mindset or Personal Growth Mentor
- What They Offer: Help with shifting your mindset, overcoming limiting beliefs, and building emotional resilience.
- Why They're Important: Entrepreneurship is as much a mental game as it is a logistical one. These mentors help you navigate self-doubt, manage fear, and build confidence.
- How to Find Them: Look for personal development coaches, therapists, or mindset-focused individuals like life coaches or breathwork facilitators.

Before making my leap, I worked with a coach who taught me how to identify and reframe my limiting beliefs. For example, I believed that failure was something to avoid at all costs. This mentor showed me that failure is just feedback—an opportunity to learn and grow. That mindset shift made all the difference.

3. Business Operations Mentor
- What They Offer: Tactical advice on the nuts and bolts of running a business, from managing finances to scaling operations.
- Why They're Important: Many entrepreneurs fail because they lack operational know-how. These mentors help you navigate financial planning, team management, and legal structures.
- How to Find Them: Seek out successful business owners, consultants, or even online mentors through platforms like SCORE or local business development centers.

When I was setting up my business, I connected with a mentor who taught me the importance of tracking key metrics like acquisition costs and case value. They helped me implement systems to ensure my firm was profitable from day one, and their guidance saved me years of trial and error.

4. Strategic Mentor
- What They Offer: Big-picture thinking and guidance on long-term decisions.
- Why They're Important: Strategy mentors help you avoid short-sighted decisions and keep you focused on the ultimate vision.
- How to Find Them: Look for seasoned entrepreneurs or executives who have successfully scaled businesses and can offer insights into long-term growth.

A strategic mentor helped me navigate one of the most difficult decisions in my career—whether to expand my firm into a new state. Their advice to focus on my core competencies first saved me from overextending too soon. Instead, I built a solid foundation before scaling.

Finding the Right Mentor

You might not need four different mentors. Some individuals can fulfill multiple roles. The key is finding someone who resonates with your values, understands your vision, and has the expertise to guide you. Here are the qualities to look for in a mentor:

- A proven track record in their field
- A willingness to challenge you and hold you accountable
- The ability to listen and understand your unique goals
- Alignment with your core values and vision

What a Mentor Can Do for You (and What You Must Do for Yourself)

Mentors are incredible guides, but they can't do the work for you. Here's what to expect:

- What Your Mentor Can Do: Provide insights, challenge your thinking, connect you with resources, and keep you accountable.
- What You Must Do: Show up prepared, be willing to learn, and take ownership of your journey. The leap is yours to make.

Investing in Yourself and Your Jump

Hiring a coach or mentor often comes with a financial investment. It's tempting to hesitate, but here's the truth: investing in yourself is the best investment you'll ever make. A mentor's guidance can save you years of costly mistakes and help you reach your goals faster.

Questions to Ask a Potential Mentor

Before committing to a mentor, ask yourself and them:

1. What specific experience do they have in my field?
2. Can they challenge me and provide honest feedback?
3. Do they align with my values and vision?
4. What kind of support will they offer (e.g., regular meetings, ad-hoc guidance)?
5. Are they genuinely invested in my success?

Attend networking events, join entrepreneurial communities, and reach out to people you admire to find mentors. It's also important to surround yourself with accountability partners who will cheer you on and challenge you when needed. I also highly advise you not to wait for the perfect mentor. Start with someone who can guide you where you are now.

Upgrading for the Next Stage: Mentors, Talent, and Mindset

Growth in business and life is a journey of constant evolution. As you climb higher, you'll find that the people, strategies, and even mindsets that got you to this point may not take you further. Growth requires not only new skills but also new relationships. This section explores how to upgrade your mentors, your internal talent, and your mindset to align with your next level of success.

Upgrading Your Mentor

It's critical to understand that the mentor who helped you reach $1 million in revenue is often not the one who will guide you to $10 million or beyond. Growth requires new perspectives, and the advice that got you through one stage of your business may not apply to the next.

Key Considerations for Upgrading Your Mentor:

1. **Alignment with Your Goals**
    Ask yourself, *Has this person been where I am trying to go?* The most valuable mentor is someone who has navigated the challenges of the level you're striving to reach.

2. **Growth Beyond Comfort Zones**
    The right mentor challenges your thinking, encourages you to confront limiting beliefs, and pushes you into new, unfamiliar territory. If your mentor's insights start to feel repetitive, it's a sign to seek someone who operates at a higher level.

3. **Scaling Expertise**
    A mentor who excels at startup strategies may lack the knowledge to guide you through scaling. Similarly, someone focused on scaling may not understand early-stage challenges. Find a mentor whose expertise matches your immediate needs.

My Journey with Mentors

My first mentor was my old boss and some of the senior people at his firm. They offered invaluable insight into making me a better lawyer, and my boss's approach to running the firm—along with the responsibility I had over my division—taught me a lot about business. My dad was also a mentor. He had run a business himself, but it never produced over a million in revenue.

When I opened my own firm, I hit a million in revenue in my first year, but without the mentorship of my old boss, I found myself in the dark, struggling to build scalable systems. That's when I began seeking out summits and seminars, soaking up lessons, and picking and choosing what would work for my business.

I was also fortunate to partner with someone ahead of me in many areas. We leaned on each other and continually pushed ourselves to learn and grow. But even with books and shared wisdom, I realized very few resources are designed to guide someone with over a million in revenue. To address this gap, I sought out business coaching and brought in a consultant who had already been where I wanted to go.

We also made significant upgrades internally. For example, we hired an HR director with experience at a Fortune 500 company and worked with experts who specialized in scaling businesses to $20 million and beyond. In the process, I had to make tough decisions, including letting go of people who didn't have the skills or growth mindset to help us achieve our goals.

The principles of upgrading mentors and talent applied not only to my firm but also to my med spa business, which is on track to hit $1 million in revenue. In this venture, I've acted as a mentor to my business partner, who achieved $500,000 in her first year—an incredible milestone in an industry where it typically takes three years to turn a profit. By the time this book is published, she'll likely have surpassed the $1 million mark.

You aren't leaving those people behind; you're just creating space so you can grow into what you are dreaming.

Upgrading Internal Talent

The team that helped you build a $1 million business might not be the team to scale to $20 million or $50 million. Growth demands systems, specialized expertise, and leadership at a higher level.

- **Systems Over Hustle:** You'll need people who can create and manage systems, not just execute tasks.
- **Specialized Expertise:** As your challenges become more complex, hire people with skills tailored to your needs at scale.

- **Leadership:** Invest in leaders who can manage teams, drive innovation, and align with your vision.

Just like with mentors, upgrading internal talent is about aligning your team with the next phase of your business. Sometimes, that means hiring new people, and sometimes, it means letting go of those who aren't growing with you.

Confronting Impostor Syndrome During Growth

As you upgrade your mentors and talent, you may feel out of place. That feeling of being surrounded by people who seem more accomplished is not a sign of inadequacy—it's proof that you're pushing into new territory. Growth requires discomfort, and these moments are invitations to expand your self-perception.

Why Discomfort Is a Sign of Progress

When you feel out of place, it's a signal that you're breaking free from your comfort zone. True growth happens here. Instead of resisting the discomfort, embrace it as a natural part of evolving into your next level.

My Experience with Impostor Syndrome

I've faced impostor syndrome many times in my career. Early on, I masked it with alcohol or what I thought of as "social courage." In rooms full of accomplished individuals, I leaned on small talk or a drink to ignore my feelings of inadequacy. But masking the discomfort only delayed my growth. When I finally allowed myself to sit with that feeling and reflect on its source, I began to evolve. I learned to own my place in those rooms, recognizing that the discomfort was a sign of progress, not failure.

Strategies for Overcoming Impostor Syndrome

1. **Acknowledge the Feeling:** Accept discomfort as a sign of growth. The nerves you feel aren't inadequacy; they're a signal that you're leveling up.

2. **Revisit Your Mental Resume:** Reflect on your accomplishments. You're in the room because you've earned it. Your track record is proof of your readiness for the next challenge.

3. **Challenge Limiting Beliefs:** Use tools from Chapter Six to reframe your thoughts. Replace "I don't belong here" with "I'm here because I've grown, and I'm ready for this."

4. **Embrace the Growth Mindset:** Discomfort is a catalyst for transformation. The feeling of being unqualified fades as you adapt and grow into your new environment.

5. **Trust the Process:** You're exactly where you're supposed to be. That uneasy feeling is there to guide you, not to hold you back. Trust that leaning into discomfort is shaping you into the person you need to become—but never forget that you're not starting from zero. You are already worthy. Mentors, upgraded teams, and new stages of growth don't add value to who you are—they simply help you express more of what's already inside you.

CHAPTER TWELVE

THE JUMP METHOD FOR SCALING AND RUNNING YOUR BUSINESS

SCALING YOUR BUSINESS AFTER MAKING THE LEAP IS ABOUT more than growth; it's about creating alignment, fostering a strong culture, and building a legacy where excellence thrives. The JUMP Method—**Justify Your Why, Uncover Limiting Beliefs, Mindset Shift, and Planning**—offers a roadmap for scaling your business while staying true to your vision. This chapter brings together all the tools and lessons needed to guide your business to its next level.

Justify Your Why: Aligning Vision and Purpose

Your *why* is the foundation of your business. It's what drives every decision, inspires your team, and ensures alignment throughout the organization. Without a clearly communicated and lived why, your business risks stagnating or growing in directions that don't serve your long-term vision.

Communicating Your Why

Your why must go beyond financial goals—it should align your personal mission with your business vision. For example, when I hired a new attorney, I told him, *I'll push you to become exactly what you dream for yourself, and in return, I ask that you push me to be the best dad I can be.* This wasn't just a motivational speech; it reflected our firm's culture of personal and professional growth.

To justify your why, ask:

- Why does your business exist beyond profitability?
- How does your vision inspire your team to bring their best selves to work?
- Are your systems and decisions aligned with your purpose?

When your team connects with your why, they're not just working for a paycheck—they're part of a mission.

Goal Setting with Visionary Leadership

Visionary leadership goes beyond managing your team; it's about inspiring them to see how their goals align with your organization's purpose. When employees feel connected to a larger vision, they're more engaged, motivated, and empowered to excel.

How to Set Goals with Visionary Leadership:

1. **Start with the Why:** Begin by sharing your company's vision and how their role contributes to the big picture.
2. **Co-Create Goals:** Ask employees about their professional and personal aspirations. Align their goals with your company's mission.
3. **Tie Goals to Growth:** Help them see how achieving their goals contributes to their personal and professional development.
4. **Break Goals into Steps:** Develop actionable milestones to make their goals achievable.
5. **Focus on Strengths:** Position team members in roles where they can excel naturally.

6. One of my attorneys wanted to oversee pre-suit operations across multiple states. Instead of simply assigning more cases, we created a roadmap for her success:

- Mastering pre-suit processes
- Taking bar exams in key jurisdictions
- Improving client satisfaction scores

This approach tied her personal growth to the company's mission, creating alignment and motivation.

The Ripple Effect of Genius

When your team operates in their zones of genius, your why becomes a lived reality. The ripple effects include:

- **Increased Engagement:** Employees feel connected to their work and purpose.
- **Enhanced Collaboration:** Teams complement each other's strengths, creating synergy.
- **Improved Results:** Aligning tasks with strengths boosts efficiency and outcomes.

Uncover Limiting Beliefs: Removing Barriers to Growth

Scaling your business often requires letting go of limiting beliefs that hold you back. These beliefs can appear as fear, insecurity, or attachment to familiar systems that no longer serve you.

Breaking Old Patterns

When I started my business, I unknowingly recreated many of the same systems and culture I had left behind. I compensated based on settlements, celebrated transactional benchmarks, and even allowed a drinking culture to emerge. It wasn't until our first Christmas party, when I looked around and saw how familiar it all felt, that I realized I was repeating the past. I had outgrown those systems, but I hadn't fully left them behind.

Breaking the cycle of familiarity means:

1. **Reflecting on Your Habits:** Are your systems aligned with your unique vision, or are they based on what feels comfortable?
2. **Embracing Change:** Be willing to create something new, even if it feels uncertain.
3. **Redefining Success:** Shift from transactional achievements to long-term, purpose-driven goals.

Knowing Your Worth

One of the most insidious limiting beliefs is undervaluing yourself. If you don't believe in your worth, it will affect every-thing—from how you price your services to how you negotiate deals. Many of us carry stories about success being tied to struggle or money being scarce. These beliefs create ceilings on what we allow ourselves to achieve.

What beliefs about money, success, or self-worth are hold-ing you back? For example, if you think, *I'm not ready to charge more,* challenge that narrative. Start showing up as the person you want to become. Charge what your work is worth, even if it feels uncomfortable at first. And use rejections or setbacks as lessons, not reflections of your value.

When you know your worth, you create space for growth and attract opportunities that align with your vision. Once your limiting beliefs are clear, the next shift is in your mindset. It's one thing to identify your old stories, but real growth comes when you reclaim your role as the creator of your outcomes.

Mindset Shift

The way you approach challenges as a leader will define the culture and trajectory of your business. Scaling a business requires shifting from a **victim mentality**—blaming external circumstances—to a **creator mentality**, where you take full responsibility for every outcome. This shift is driven by two critical concepts: **Owning the Outcome** and **Understanding the Role of Confirmation Bias.**

Owning the Outcome

As a leader, you must take 100 percent responsibility for your business and your team. Success isn't about pointing fingers or finding someone to blame when things go wrong. It's about holding yourself accountable for every outcome.

When your team fails, it reflects gaps in your leadership—whether in setting clear expectations, providing necessary tools, or making tough but essential decisions. Owning the outcome doesn't mean blaming yourself for everything; it means recognizing that you have the power to influence every aspect of your business.

For example:

If a team member isn't performing, ask yourself:
- *Did I provide adequate training?*
- *Did I set clear goals and expectations?*
- *Did I give them the tools and support needed to succeed?*
If your business isn't meeting its goals, reflect:
- *Have I aligned the team with the company's vision?*
- *Am I focusing on solutions rather than dwelling on problems?*
- *Am I making decisions that prioritize growth and alignment?*

This concept is a powerful antidote to the victim mentality, which focuses on external circumstances—bad luck, poor timing, or someone else's mistakes—as excuses for failure. True leadership requires shifting from asking, *Why is this happening to me?* to asking, *What can I do to improve the situation?*

When you embrace this mindset, you empower your team to do the same. Accountability becomes the standard, creating an environment where excellence thrives. Owning the outcome also means making tough decisions. If someone on your team isn't living up to the vision, it's your responsibility to either develop them or help them find a better fit. Letting someone go isn't a failure; it's an act of alignment with your purpose and theirs.

The Role of Confirmation Bias

Confirmation bias plays a powerful role in shaping your mindset. If you view every problem as catastrophic, your brain will seek evidence to reinforce that belief, magnifying failures and limiting progress. Conversely, if you train your brain to focus on growth and opportunity, confirmation bias will work in your favor, highlighting solutions and driving momentum.

I once worked with a leader who was fixated on an employee's mistakes. Her confirmation bias reinforced the belief that he wasn't capable, blinding her to his growth or potential. Through coaching, we reframed her perspective by focusing on his strengths. Once she shifted her focus, we repositioned him in a role where he thrived—and he became one of our top performers.

How to Leverage Confirmation Bias:

1. **Reframe Challenges:** Instead of fixating on what's broken, focus on what's working and how it can be

improved.

2. **Model Optimism:** Your mindset as a leader sets the tone for your team. When you approach challenges with optimism, your team will follow suit.

3. **Celebrate Progress:** Acknowledge wins, no matter how small. Celebrating progress creates momentum and reinforces a culture of growth.

In recognizing and shifting confirmation bias, you can turn challenges into opportunities and create a mindset that drives your business forward.

Rejecting the Victim Mentality

Owning the outcome and leveraging confirmation bias are antidotes to the victim mentality that keeps many leaders stuck. A victim mentality thrives on blame and excuses:

- *"This team member is just lazy."*
- *"If the market weren't so competitive, we'd be doing better."*
- *"I can't succeed because no one on my team is stepping up."*

These excuses might feel valid in the moment, but they strip you of the power to create meaningful change. Blame becomes a crutch, distracting you from opportunities for growth.

The Creator Mentality Shift

Rejecting the victim mentality doesn't mean taking on blame for everything; it means taking responsibility for what you can control. This shift liberates you to lead with clarity, purpose, and confidence. Instead of focusing on why something failed, ask yourself:

- *What role did I play in this outcome?*
- *What changes can I make to improve the situation?*
- *What steps can I take to prevent this in the future?*

When you take ownership, you shift from a reactive mindset to a proactive one. This empowers you to address problems head-on and build a culture of accountability within your organization.

A Story of Ownership in Action

Early in my career, I struggled with holding the intake team accountable for missed leads. My initial reaction was frustration: *Why don't they care as much as I do?* I blamed them for the lost opportunities and told myself they were the problem.

Then I realized I wasn't living by the principle of owning the outcome. When I took a step back, I asked myself hard questions:

- *Did I provide proper training?*
- *Did I establish clear expectations for lead management?*
- *Did I create systems to help them succeed?*

The answers were no. I hadn't equipped them for success. Taking responsibility led me to redesign the training process, improve communication, and implement better tracking systems. Within weeks, the team's performance improved dramatically. The problem wasn't "lazy employees." It was a gap in leadership.

The Ripple Effect of Ownership

When you model ownership and apply the lessons of confirmation bias, your team follows suit. They stop blaming others or external factors and start taking responsibility for their own roles. This shift creates a culture where accountability isn't feared, but it's embraced, and everyone works together toward a shared vision.

When you reject the victim mentality and fully embrace ownership, you unlock the ability to lead with confidence and clarity. You stop reacting to circumstances and start creating the outcomes you desire. With a new mindset in place, the final step in the JUMP Method is about turning clarity into action. That means planning—deliberately, consistently, and with the systems that allow your vision to scale.

Planning: From Vision to Execution

Once your culture is aligned and your standards are high, it's time to ground your vision in action. The inner work—clarifying your why, uncovering limiting beliefs, and shifting your mindset—has prepared you for what comes next: execution. Planning is what transforms your leap into something sustainable.

You don't scale and then create systems—you scale because you create systems. Great businesses don't run on hope, motivation, or talent alone. They run on rhythms, measurements, and intentional design.

This is where Planning completes the JUMP Method: Justify, Uncover, Mindset, and now, Planning. It's the bridge between your why and the daily actions that bring it to life.

Strategic Planning Rhythms: Ninety-Day to Long-Term

A plan without cadence is just a wish. I run my businesses using three strategic planning windows:

- **Long-Term (Three to Five Years):** This is your vision horizon. How many clients, patients, or cases do you want? What kind of impact will you be having?
- **Annual Planning:** Your yearly goals should align with your long-term vision and translate into specific revenue, hiring, marketing, or operational milestones.
- **Ninety-Day Sprints:** This is where the real work happens.

Break annual goals into ninety-day rocks—concrete, measurable, and owned by a person. Every quarter, we identify top priorities that move the needle and eliminate distractions.

- **Weekly Scorecards:** Weekly accountability ensures that no one is surprised when a rock isn't hit. Each department or pod owns two to four weekly KPIs that tie directly to a ninety-day rock.

In our law firm, one of our ninety-day rocks was to reduce pre-litigation cycle time. The weekly scorecard for that team tracked:

- Insurance demand submission rate.
- Case-to-litigation conversion rate.
- Medical record retrieval lag time.

In our med spa, the quarterly rock was to increase rebooking by 20 percent. The weekly scorecard tracked:

- Rebooking rate.
- Cancellation-to-rebook conversion.
- Average time between treatments.

Forecasting Cash and Capacity

Vision without cash is a hallucination.
You need to know:

- How much cash you have.
- How much is coming in.
- When it's coming in.
- What your team can handle.

From Bottlenecks to Breakthroughs

Every system you build will eventually expose its own inefficiencies. Planning isn't just about setting goals; it's about tracking **what's slowing things down**.

Here's a four-step process we use to identify and solve bottlenecks—something you can apply in any business:

The Bottleneck Breakthrough Tool

Step	What to Do	Example – Law Firm	Example – Med Spa
1. Identify the Symptom	Look at lagging results.	Cases are sitting too long in pre-lit.	Rebooking rate is below industry benchmarks.
2. Ask Why (Root Cause)	Peel back the issue.	Prelit attorneys are incentivized to settle but not to move cases into litigation.	Front desk isn't trained to reschedule next appointments at checkout.
3. Match to the Right Fix	Connect the issue to a system or training problem.	Adjust compensation to include bonuses for moving files to litigation.	Train front desk on rebooking scripts and track individual rebooking rates.
4. Take Leadership Action	Implement and inspect.	Weekly meeting: Track proposals for settlement, depositions set, complaints filed.	Weekly report: Percent rebooked before leaving, percent returned within thirty days.

In our firm, we noticed cases were stalling in pre-litigation. Upon investigation, we realized our attorneys were being incentivized only on settlements, so they were avoiding the friction of transitioning to litigation. We updated our comp model to reward case progression, not just outcomes. This small shift unlocked velocity and improved client outcomes.

But culture isn't enough.

Once the foundation is laid, the real danger starts creeping in—hidden traps that threaten to collapse your momentum under the weight of complexity. This next phase requires discipline, not just vision.

Hidden Traps That Can Break Your Jump

Between $5 and $10 million, growth starts to feel like quicksand. Your revenue rises. Your team expands. You start adding departments, managers, systems, and layers of structure. On the surface, it looks like you're scaling, but underneath, profit vanishes. Everything starts to feel more complicated, not more efficient.

This is what Greg Crabtree calls "The Black Hole."[5] Doug Tatum calls it "No Man's Land."[6] Startup Genome found that 74 percent of startups fail because they scale too early, before validating that they should.[7] This is the second leap. The first is jumping from safety into entrepreneurship. The second is jumping from hustle to real company. And that second leap? It doesn't reward ego. It rewards discipline.

The temptation is to fix chaos by throwing people at it— hiring fast, layering software, or chasing systems before process. But most of those moves only add complexity and slowly bleed your business.

You go from focused growth to bloated teams and flat cash flow. And the scariest part? It looks like scaling—but profit quietly vanishes.

The lesson? Don't scale out of boredom. Don't scale out of comparison. Scale when your momentum demands it, not when your ego does.

Flywheel Versus Doom Loop

Flywheel Path:
Clear focus → Consistent execution → Momentum → Repeatable profit → Strategic structure

Doom Loop Path:
Impulse hire → Confused operations → Complexity → Burnout → Panic fixes → More hires

JUMP Checkpoint: Strategic Change Filter

Before you make a major change—like hiring new staff, buying software, restructuring teams, or expanding locations—run it through this simple but ruthless filter:

- Will this directly increase sales or client experience right now?
- Can I afford it without dipping below 15 percent profit?
- Am I fixing a real bottleneck or avoiding a harder conversation?

If the change won't create leverage, wait. Simplicity beats complexity. Always.

The businesses that make it through this squeeze aren't the ones that move the fastest. They're the ones who know what not to do.

They understand that building with intention matters more than reacting to every opportunity or problem.

Build Lift Before You Build the Plane

In the beginning, your only job is to sell. Until money comes in the door, you don't have a business—you have an expensive hobby.

As Michael Masterson writes in *Ready, Fire, Aim,* "The most important task in the infancy stage is to sell, sell, sell."

Don't build your SOPs, team, or tech stack until you have customers and cash flow. Webvan scaled logistics before sales and died. Stripe and Airbnb knocked on doors and integrated users manually. That's the playbook.

Before investing in a new hire, system, or process, ask yourself:

Will this help us sell more right now?

If the answer is no, wait.

Visual Timeline

$0–$1M: Founder = Chief Sales Officer

$1–5M: Build repeatable sales engine

$5–10M: Add layers of structure (with caution)

$10M+: Scale what already works

If you can't sell it, don't build it!

See the Terrain Clearly Before You Leap

I've had to look at bank accounts, case metrics, and hiring flops that made me question everything. There were times when the vision felt blurry and the pressure felt personal.

But I never let brutal facts crush the vision.

Facing reality is not about being pessimistic. It's about being responsible. It's about having the maturity to say, "This isn't working," and then doing something about it. Whether it was a marketing strategy that flopped, a leader who didn't work out, or a period when revenue stalled, I had to stay grounded in facts while refusing to give up on the future.

It's easy to fantasize your way into chaos. It's also easy to get so bogged down in problems that you forget why you started. Leadership requires that you hold both: the truth of where you are and the belief in where you're going.

That's how you move forward. That's how you stay alive. Reality without resilience is just defeat.

Lead with Vision; Let Go with Trust

Jim Collins said it best: Great companies don't start with a grand vision. They start with the right people.

First who, then what.

I used to think the most important decisions were about strategy, pricing, and systems. But those decisions only work if the people executing them believe in the mission and take ownership of the outcome.

It wasn't about resumes—it was about alignment. About energy. The wrong person in the right role is still the wrong fit. Hiring is more than a transaction. It's an invitation onto your ship.

And I used to think that if I wasn't involved in everything, things would fall apart. But the truth was, things couldn't truly come together until I got out of the way.

Delegation isn't just about efficiency. It's about growth—yours and your team's. You build systems so others can take ownership. You hire leaders so they can lead. You step back, not because you're less needed but because your value is now in vision, not volume.

That's leadership: setting the course, defining the culture, and choosing people who want to row with you, not against you.

When you get the right people on the bus and let them drive, your company doesn't just grow—it gains momentum.

You Were Wired for Flight

Some people find peace in routine. Others find peace in progress.

I used to think something was wrong with me. I'd hit goals. I'd outperform my peers. But a few days later, I'd feel this deep emptiness. Almost like I had nothing left to chase. I remember once crushing a quarterly goal, walking into my office, sitting down—and staring at the wall for fifteen minutes, completely hollow. No joy. No fire. Just the sinking feeling that it wasn't enough. That I wasn't enough.

It wasn't until I discovered how I was wired that it all made sense: I'm not broken. I'm driven.

As Dr. Doug Brackmann writes in Driven, some people are biologically built for novelty, intensity, and tension. They need challenge. They crave purpose. And without it, they don't just lose motivation—they self-destruct.

The brain of a driven person isn't satisfied by checking boxes. It needs a mission. It needs meaning.

We're dopamine-fueled machines. We thrive on tension, traction, and creation. That's why comfort zones feel suffocating. That's why traditional career paths often feel like cages.

If that sounds like you, here's what you need to know:

- You are not broken.
- You don't need to be fixed.
- You need a path that matches your intensity.

You were wired for the jump.

Because when you stop trying to conform—and start building something that actually excites you—you stop feeling like a misfit and start feeling like a creator.

That shift in identity is what allows you to build something big, bold, and meaningful.

So don't shrink to fit the mold. Break the mold to fit your mission.

Because in the end, scaling isn't about becoming someone else; it's about finally building something that fits who you've been all along

Designing Systems That Scale

To truly scale, your systems must increase both efficiency and service. That's what we call **White Glove at Scale**.

We created a **tiered communication system** to ensure every client receives proactive updates based on their case stage. This wasn't just for client experience; it allowed us to monitor whether key actions were happening on time:

- Are insurance demands being sent out within thirty days?
- Are complaints being filed fast enough?
- Are depositions and mediations being scheduled early?
- Are medical bills and records being returned fast enough?
- Is the case being noticed for trial if it's not settling?

In our med spa, the same idea applies:

- Are patients rebooked before leaving?
- Are treatment plans documented and followed?
- Are consultations being converted?
- Are revenue-generating treatments scheduled consistently?

When something breaks down—whether it's a complaint not being filed or a patient not returning—it tells a story. A complaint that wasn't filed might mean a paralegal is overloaded or an attorney hasn't reviewed the case. A patient not rebooked might mean the provider didn't build rapport or the front desk skipped the close.

We don't just manage people—we manage systems. This creates **visibility** and allows us to act early instead of reacting late.

The Final Link: Your Why in Action

All the planning, forecasting, and dashboards mean nothing if they don't connect back to your why.

- Why do you want to scale?
- What kind of experience do you want your clients—or patients—to have?
- What kind of life do you want your team to live?

When you build systems that create clarity, eliminate friction, and serve the people who trust you, you're not just running a business. You're building a legacy.

Planning is where your purpose meets the real world.

Vision and Culture in Partnership

Scaling a business requires more than a visionary leader; it requires visionary collaboration. At our firm, my law partner and I work together to define and evolve our shared vision. While I naturally gravitate toward systems, growth, and execution, he focuses heavily on culture, communication, and the human side of leadership. He often says, "The business will only grow as much as we do," and he lives that truth by constantly developing our people, hiring intentionally, and creating a workplace where high performers thrive.

We challenge each other to think bigger, lead better, and never lose sight of the values that drive our business. This partnership between vision and culture is what allows us to scale with both heart and precision.

This shared leadership model works because we focus on more than just performance metrics. We build from the top line—not just in dollars, but in **culture**, **vision**, and **values**.

Top Line First: Culture, Vision, and the Rest Will Follow

In business, especially in law, it's easy to become obsessed with the bottom line—settlement numbers, margins, revenue targets. And while those things matter, they're not the foundation. If you want to build something that actually lasts—something you're proud of—you have to look upstream. Not at outcomes, but at what creates them. When I started building this firm, I knew I couldn't do it alone—not just because of the scale of the work but because I needed someone who believed in what we were building as much as I did. That's where my law partner came in.

We complement each other in all the right ways. I focus on the systems—the infrastructure, automation, marketing, and scale. He focuses on the people—on culture, on HR, and on making sure our team feels supported, aligned, and ready to show up fully every day. He's also a trial lawyer, and he tries cases when the moment calls for it, but his true superpower is how deeply he invests in the team.

While I focus most of my attention on building the machine, he's been building the human engine that runs it.

We aligned early on around a shared philosophy: if we get the top line right—the vision, the team, the values—the bottom line will take care of itself.

Steve Jobs said it perfectly:

"If you take care of the top line, the bottom line will follow."

In our world, the top line isn't just revenue. It's culture. It's leadership. It's the emotional climate of your company. We've learned that when the team is thriving, clients are served better. When values are clear, decisions are easier. When the internal structure is aligned, performance becomes inevitable.

Our employee retention rate is incredible, not just because of systems but because of the culture my partner cultivates.

From the moment someone joins our team, he sends them a personal message, gets them branded swag, and makes sure they're welcomed by the rest of the firm.

But it goes deeper than that. I once watched him sit down with a new employee and begin the conversation with a single question: "How can I support you?" Then he listened, not just to their goals at the firm but to who they wanted to become as a person.

When one team member shared that completing a 5K was on their personal goal list, my partner didn't just cheer them on—he arranged a firm-wide 5K, got everyone on Strava, and created a wave of encouragement that rippled through the team. That's who he is.

He doesn't just build culture. He lives it—one relationship, one gesture, one act of support at a time

You can always push for better financials. But unless your people are on board—unless the internal foundation is strong—those wins won't last. Culture isn't soft; it's structural. It's the compound interest of how people feel about where they work, who they work with, and what they're building together.

Reflection Prompt: Culture

Who's tending to your culture while you build your systems? Are you investing in the emotional infrastructure of your business, or are you counting on profit to outrun misalignment?

Transition: From Vision to Vigilance

But culture isn't enough.

Once the foundation is laid, the real work begins—developing your people, not just your systems. It's not structure that scales a business. It's leaders who own the mission, think critically, and help drive it forward. This next phase requires discipline, not just inspiration.

Making the jump from aligned culture to empowered execution starts by building leaders who think, act, and grow with you.

Developing People, Not Just Systems

Once your vision and culture are aligned at the leadership level, the real magic happens through individual growth.

Systems provide the framework, but it's people who bring your vision to life, one action, one decision, one relationship at a time.

This section isn't just about organizational culture. It's about how you intentionally develop the individuals on your team. A high-performing team doesn't happen by accident. It's built through meaningful relationships, high expectations, and leadership rooted in authenticity and purpose.

Great leaders don't just design systems—they develop people. As a visionary, your role goes beyond managing workflows or chasing KPIs. It's about creating an environment where team members feel seen, challenged, and empowered to grow. That means shifting from a transactional mindset to a transformational one.

When you focus on developing people, you don't just build a stronger organization—you build a legacy.

At our firm, this philosophy comes to life through the work of our HR Director. She collaborates with leadership to ensure every team member feels supported, challenged, and aligned with our mission. From performance reviews to professional development, her role isn't just administrative—it's transformational.

Acting as a Visionary Leader

Visionary leadership starts with recognizing that each person on your team has unique potential. Your job is to help them uncover that potential and align it with the organization's goals. This requires listening, asking the right questions, and co-creating a plan for their development.

For example, as I write this, I recall a recent conversation with a new hire. I asked him about his vision, not just for his role but for his career. Together, we developed a plan to help him achieve it. Part of that plan involves settling cases, which is critical to his immediate success. But settling cases is just one piece of a larger puzzle. The bigger picture is about helping him become the best version of himself, which, in turn, moves our organization closer to its vision.

Visionary leaders don't see people as cogs in a machine. They see them as partners in building something extraordinary. By helping your team members define their "why" and connecting it to the organization's mission, you unlock levels of commitment and performance that no system alone could achieve.

Being a visionary leader also means embracing gratitude. It's not just about recognizing what's going well; it's about appreciating everything that has brought you to this point, even the challenges. Gratitude keeps you grounded and strengthens your ability to inspire others.

For me, gratitude begins with acknowledging the people and experiences that shaped my journey. I am thankful for every single person who doubted me, for they gave me the fuel to prove them wrong. I am thankful for my former boss, who unknowingly pushed me to become more than I ever thought I could be. I am thankful for hitting rock bottom because it was there that I found the clarity and strength to rise again.

I am also deeply grateful for my business partners, who believed in me and encouraged me to create in my zone of genius. I am thankful for my wife, who stood by my side through the highs and lows, never wavering in her support. I am thankful for my daughters—Charley, who reminds me to find joy, and Noah, whose smile melts my heart every single day.

When you lead with gratitude, it changes how you show up for your team. It allows you to see their potential, not just as professionals but as people. Gratitude connects you to your purpose and theirs, creating an environment where everyone can thrive. It's a key ingredient in visionary leadership, one that transforms a workplace into a shared mission with limitless possibilities.

Building a Culture of Loyalty

I've always believed that a leader's actions set the tone for the entire team. When people see that you're willing to go above and beyond for them, they'll often respond in kind.

My personal assistant once drove through the night so I could save money on a flight and get enough rest before an important meeting. She didn't do this because it was part of her job description. She did it because we had built a relationship of loyalty and trust. She knew I would go to the same lengths for her if the roles were reversed.

That kind of commitment doesn't just come from hiring the right people—it comes from creating a culture where people feel valued and supported. When your team knows that you're invested in their success, they'll invest in the organization's success with equal passion.

Fostering a High-Performance Culture

Mediocre performers don't thrive in environments built for high achievers. High-performing cultures are created intentionally, with clarity, accountability, and alignment to a shared vision as their foundation. Every person in your organization should understand how their role contributes to the larger mission and feel empowered to excel within that framework.

However, maintaining a high-performance culture requires courage. It's not enough to hire great people; you also need to ensure that every member of your team consistently contributes to the organization's goals. This sometimes means making tough decisions, including letting go of individuals who are not aligned with your vision.

Letting Go of Mediocrity

Holding on to mediocrity often stems from limiting beliefs, such as:
- "What if I can't replace them?"
- "What if letting them go causes problems?"
- "I don't want to be seen as difficult or demanding."

These thoughts are rooted in fear and scarcity, but they don't serve you, your team, or your business. Reframing these beliefs is essential. Letting go of mediocrity is not about being harsh or unforgiving; it's an act of service. When you allow underperformance to persist, it drags down the entire team, creating frustration and misalignment. By making the tough calls, you uphold your organization's standards and open the door for someone better suited to the role.

Reframe these beliefs:
- Instead of "What if I can't replace them?", think "Replacing them creates an opportunity to bring in someone who elevates the team."
- Instead of "What if letting them go causes problems?", think "Holding on to them causes more problems in the long run."
- Instead of "I don't want to be seen as difficult," think "Leadership means prioritizing the vision and holding the team accountable."

Every decision you make should align with your *why* and your purpose. Letting go of mediocrity is not about punishment; it's about creating space for excellence.

Connecting Back to the JUMP Method

The same principles that helped you make the jump—Justifying Your Why, Uncovering Limiting Beliefs, Shifting Your Mindset, and Planning—are just as critical when you're learning to fly. Your *why* acts as your compass, guiding every decision. If any part of your business or team isn't aligned with that *why*, it's time to make a change.

- **Justify Your Why:** Why does your team exist? How does each member contribute to the vision?
- **Uncover Limiting Beliefs:** Are fears or insecurities holding you back from addressing underperformance?
- **Shift Your Mindset:** Recognize that hard decisions are part of great leadership.
- **Plan:** Develop a clear process for evaluating team members, coaching where possible, and transitioning where necessary.

Building a high-performance culture isn't about being perfect; it's about staying true to your vision and ensuring your team reflects that commitment.

Practical Business Step

Here's a step-by-step approach to foster a high-performance culture:

1. **Conduct a Team Audit**
   - **List your team members**: Evaluate their alignment with your vision and purpose. Are they contributing to your goals or holding the team back?

- **Identify high performers**: Highlight those who consistently exceed expectations and contribute positively to the culture.
- **Spot areas for development:** Note where additional coaching or support is needed to elevate performance.

2. Develop Your Team

- **Meet with each team member**: Discuss their goals and aspirations. How do their personal ambitions align with the organization's vision?
- **Align objectives**: Co-create a plan that helps them grow while contributing to the business's success.
- **Provide mentorship and resources**: Offer training, tools, and guidance to help them excel. A strong leader invests in their team's development.

3. Address Mediocrity

- **Reflect on limiting beliefs**: Ask yourself if fear or emotional attachment is preventing you from making necessary changes.
- **Create a coaching plan**: If someone is underperforming, outline specific steps to help them improve.
- **Transition when necessary**: If coaching doesn't yield results, be clear, kind, and firm about transitioning them out of the organization.

4. Build a High-Performance Culture

- **Celebrate wins**: Recognize and reward high achievers. Public acknowledgment reinforces the behaviors you want to see.
- **Set clear expectations**: Ensure every team member knows what's expected of them and the standards they're held to.

- **Hold everyone accountable**: Consistency is key. High-performance cultures thrive on fairness and clarity, not favoritism or vague expectations.

The Power of Alignment

Fostering a high-performance culture isn't just about removing mediocrity; it's about creating an environment where excellence thrives. When every person on your team is aligned with your vision, the energy shifts. Productivity improves, morale soars, and the team moves forward with a shared sense of purpose.

Alignment also builds trust. When your team knows you're willing to make tough decisions to protect the vision, they'll feel more confident in their roles. They'll understand that being part of your organization means being part of something exceptional.

The Ripple Effect

By fostering a high-performance culture, you create a ripple effect that extends far beyond your immediate team. High performers inspire those around them, setting a standard of excellence that elevates the entire organization.

When you align your people, systems, and vision, you build a culture that doesn't just survive—it thrives. These culture-building strategies don't stand alone; they embody the very same JUMP principles that got you here. Let's connect the dots.

CHAPTER THIRTEEN

METRICS AND FINANCIAL RATIOS THAT ACTUALLY MATTER

MOST ENTREPRENEURS EITHER IGNORE THE NUMBERS OR drown in them.

But the secret to a scalable, profitable business isn't more data—it's knowing *which numbers to watch* and *what they actually mean.*

When you understand your margins, ratios, and velocity, you stop reacting and start *steering.*

Why Ratios Matter (but Only If You Know What You're Looking At)

Ratios are like vital signs. They give you a snapshot of how your business is functioning. But just like blood pressure or heart rate, a number alone doesn't diagnose the illness.

We had a point in our journey where gross margin, profit per employee, and even revenue looked strong, but we weren't making the money we should've been.

The real sickness? *Velocity.*

Projects weren't moving. Outcomes were delayed. Revenue was trapped in the pipeline.

The lesson? *Ratios only help if you know what they're pointing to.*

Gross Margin: Your Most Powerful—and Misunderstood—Metric

Gross margin is your first checkpoint of profitability. It tells you how much revenue is left after delivering your service—but before admin, leadership, or marketing costs.

How you define "delivery" depends on your business model.

In a Service Business (consulting, client work, legal, coaching):

Adjusted Gross Margin = (Revenue – Labor Cost to Deliver Service) ÷ Revenue

Healthy: 50–65 percent

Below 50 percent? You may be bloated, underproductive, or dragging delivery timelines.

In a Med Spa (Service + Product Hybrid):

Adjusted Gross Margin = (Revenue – Provider Labor – Product and Consumables) ÷ Revenue

Healthy: 70–80 percent

Elite: 80–85 percent

If you improve margin and profit doesn't follow, you've got a leak: waste, discounting, scheduling, or underutilized talent.

Overhead: Split It Before You Scale It

Overhead isn't the enemy—*unproductive overhead* is.

Separate your expenses into:

1. Operational Overhead

- Delivery staff
- Service tools
- Software tied directly to outcomes

Healthy: 35–40 percent of revenue

High-growth: Up to 50–55 percent temporarily

2. Non-Operational Overhead

- Leadership
- Admin
- HR, Finance, Marketing

Healthy: 15–25 percent of revenue

The 7 Core Ratios That Reveal the Truth

1. **Adjusted Gross Margin**: 50–65 percent (services), 70–85 percent (hybrid)
2. **Net Profit Margin**: 15–30 percent of revenue
3. **Profit per Employee**: $75K–$125K+
4. **Revenue per Client/Job**: Benchmark varies by model, but low-dollar churn = red flag
5. **CAC to LTV Ratio**: Aim for 3:1
6. **Operational Overhead Ratio**: 35–40 percent (steady), up to 55 percent (growth)
7. **Closure Velocity**: 5–7 percent of active inventory per month closed is healthy

Inventory, Velocity, and Growth: How Much Should You Be Closing Each Month?

If you're managing deliverables over time, your **inventory is your cash pipeline.** Whether it's client work, projects, treatments, or cases—inventory only creates value when it moves. You're not in the business of collecting potential. You're in the business of *converting* it.

Monthly Closure Rate Benchmarks

- Steady State: 5–7 percent closed monthly
- High Growth: 3–5 percent

- Stalled: Below 3 percent

Growth Stage Metrics: Know What Phase You're In

Phase 1: Build/Startup

- Low inventory
- Closure rate: 10–15 percent
- Proving model, fast delivery

Phase 2: High Growth

- Inventory balloons
- Team building ahead of revenue
- Closure percent drops, volume rises

Phase 3: Stabilization

- Systems mature
- Closure rate: 5–7 percent
- Profitability returns

Phase 4: Optimization

- Strategic hiring, clear metrics
- Velocity + quality outcomes
- You ask: How do I scale profit without scaling workload?

Metrics Are Useless Without Mindset

You can build the perfect dashboard.

Track every ratio.

Forecast, budget, optimize.

But **none of it matters** if you don't have the mindset to *face what the numbers are telling you.*

Metrics are a mirror. Mindset is the courage to look.

I remember something my dad once said:

"I don't want to go to the doctor because I'm afraid of what they'll find."

That fear—of truth, of diagnosis, of change—shows up in business, too.

I've seen people avoid their numbers for months. Others hide behind revenue while cash bleeds. Many sense the problem but avoid naming it.

The number isn't the problem. The *fear of what it means* is.

The Mindset Shift: From Performer to Pilot

Most people approach metrics with a **performer's mindset**:

"Am I doing well enough? Do these numbers make me look successful?"

But that keeps you in shame, comparison, or denial.

The shift happens when you adopt the **pilot's mindset**:

"What are these numbers telling me about where I'm going?" "What adjustments can I make?" "What am I avoiding?"

Pilots don't make it personal. They use the data to course-correct. That's what real leadership looks like.

JUMP Insight: Metrics Without Mindset Are Just Math

You can't scale what you don't understand.

You can't fix what you're afraid to face.

You can't lead what you don't measure.

My dad didn't want to go to the doctor because, deep down, he already knew something wasn't right. But he didn't want it confirmed.

I've seen entrepreneurs do the same thing with their dashboards.

Avoiding the truth delays the possibility of growth.

Metrics are your compass.

Mindset is your courage.

Leadership is your decision to look, learn, and act.

Reflection Prompt: Your Metrics Mirror

What number are you avoiding in your business right now—and what might it be trying to tell you?

- Is it your cash flow?
- Your velocity?
- Your margin?
- Your team's output?

What truth are you resisting?

What decision are you postponing?

What would change if you faced it today?

Mini Action Step

Pick one metric you've been avoiding and face it head-on.

- Pull the data.
- Ask yourself what it's trying to show you.
- Identify one system-level change you can make this week based on that insight.

The fastest growth comes when you stop avoiding the truth and start designing around it.

You've laid the foundation, aligned your culture, and installed systems that scale. But sustainable growth doesn't happen alone. In the next chapter, we'll explore how to *build leaders*, not just employees—so you can step into your next evolution without losing what makes your business great.

CHAPTER FOURTEEN

CONTINUE TO LEAP WITH FIRST STEPS

THE JUMP ISN'T A ONE-TIME EVENT. IT'S A SERIES OF LEAPS, each leading to new challenges, lessons, and opportunities for growth. The real magic of the jump lies in the continuous process of pushing past comfort zones and stepping into the unknown. Success is not a destination but a journey of self-discovery and reinvention. This chapter serves as a reminder that the journey doesn't end—it evolves. As you jump, grow, and adapt, you uncover new layers of your potential and find fresh ways to align with your passions and purpose.

The Infinite Growth Cycle

Entrepreneurship isn't a straight climb—it's a cycle.

Every milestone you reach doesn't signal an endpoint; it unlocks a new beginning. A new layer. A deeper version of who you're meant to become. I call this The Infinite Growth Cycle—the recurring loop of expansion, reflection, reinvention, and execution that defines every successful entrepreneur's journey.

This isn't a one-time transformation. It's a lifelong rhythm.

Each jump brings clarity—but also more complexity.

More questions. More responsibility. More opportunity to level up.

Growth is infinite because you are.

And with every stage, you meet a new version of yourself—one with a bigger vision, higher standards, and a deeper capacity to lead.

That sticky note used to haunt me.

Now it fuels me.

It reminds me that no one else can define my worth—or write my future.

I used to think that once I hit certain revenue goals, I'd feel "finished." But every time I achieved a milestone, I found myself asking, *What's next?* Growth isn't just about numbers; it's about becoming the person capable of reaching the next level.

The person who gets you to six figures isn't the same person who will get you to seven or eight. Each new stage of growth demands a different version of you—a version willing to let go of old habits, embrace new challenges, and grow in ways you never imagined. You have to be willing to embrace the process and trust that with each evolution, you're building the foundation for what comes next.

Navigating the Cycles of Growth

Starting a business often begins with excitement, but it inevitably leads to challenges—moments where doubt and discomfort creep in. Growth requires leaning into those cycles, creating chaos, and trusting that clarity will follow.

The first couple of months after opening my business were filled with excitement. I had an office space, two employees, and big dreams. I felt ready to take over the world. But when the phone didn't immediately start ringing, I got nervous. Then, almost overnight, the faucet turned on, and I had to figure out how to manage the influx of calls, cases, and staff. I was stressed and scared, but I leaned into the chaos. On the other side was a business that functioned well, growing revenue and providing a positive client experience. There were tough times—and there will be more—but I'm ready to embrace all of it.

Growth requires embracing discomfort. It's not about avoiding challenges but recognizing them as a necessary part of building something extraordinary.

Resilience Beyond Scaling

Scaling doesn't eliminate challenges; it creates new ones. The mindset shifts you developed in earlier stages remain critical. Reframing failure, taking ownership, and embracing growth are essential for navigating the pressures of scaling.

Failure Doesn't Exist: It's All Growth

For most people, failure is an endpoint—a red light signaling the end of the road. But failure doesn't exist in the way most people understand it. The only true failure is quitting, and when your why is strong enough, quitting isn't an option.

Failure isn't a stopping point; it's a **growth trial**. It's a stepping-stone that teaches you what doesn't work and arms you with the knowledge to move forward, smarter, stronger, and more focused.

That's all failure really is:

A growth trial—dressed in discomfort.

It may sting. It may rattle your confidence. But it's not a death sentence; it's a data point. It's where feedback becomes fuel. When you begin to expect growth trials, you stop fearing failure and start mining it for the insight that will carry you to the next level. The only real loss is failing to extract the lesson.

The Growth Trial: Failure in Disguise

Failure isn't the end. It's the experiment.
Every time you fall short, face resistance, or get knocked off course, you're not breaking down—you're stepping into a growth trial. It's a test, not a punishment. A challenge dressed in discomfort. And if you're paying attention, it's showing you exactly where your next evolution lives.

We're trained to fear failure. To avoid it. To see it as proof that we're not ready. But in reality, failure is one of the most honest teachers you'll ever have. It doesn't sugarcoat. It doesn't flatter. It reveals.

A growth trial isn't a sign you're off track; it's confirmation that you're on the edge of something new.

The mistake most people make? They confuse the pain of learning with the pain of loss. They retreat just before the shift. But if you can stay in it long enough to decode it, every failed launch, every quiet quarter, every rejected idea becomes feedback.

That's all growth really is:

Iteration fueled by insight.

So, the next time something doesn't go your way, don't ask, *"Why did this happen to me?"*

Ask, *"What part of me is this trying to upgrade?"*

Your biggest leaps often begin in your lowest moments. And when you stop seeing failure as an identity and start seeing it as a growth trial, you stop hesitating—and start adapting.

Reflection Prompt: Growth Trial

- What was your last growth trial?
- What truth did it try to teach you?
- How can you integrate that lesson into your next decision?

When I invested in marketing, I knew some campaigns would fail. And they did. Some failures were predictable, but others revealed blind spots in my strategies. Instead of giving up, I leaned into the lessons. Each failure became a growth trial that taught me how to refine my approach. Over time, I dramatically lowered case acquisition costs and built a marketing strategy that worked.

The Importance of Continual Learning

Growth doesn't end after the initial leap; it's a lifelong process. The entrepreneurial journey demands a mindset of curiosity, adaptability, and relentless self-improvement. Success comes from staying ahead—whether by learning new skills, seeking out mentors, or surrounding yourself with people who challenge and inspire you. That growth only becomes scalable when it's measured. And not all measurements are created equal.

How to Create Meaningful KPIs (Not Vanity Metrics)

Most entrepreneurs track too much—or worse, the wrong things.

They confuse motion with momentum, spreadsheets with strategy. The goal of a KPI isn't to look impressive; it's to help you make better decisions. That's it.

Here's how to build real Key Performance Indicators (KPIs) that actually move the needle:

Step 1: Know What You're Building

Start with the outcome. Ask yourself:

What does "winning" look like in the next ninety days?

- *More leads?*
- *Better client experience?*
- *Higher profit margin?*

Get specific. KPIs are useless if you don't know what they're guiding you toward.

Step 2: Identify Your Lead and Lag Indicators

Category	Lead Indicator (Drives the Result)	Lag Indicator (the Result)
Marketing	# of qualified leads generated	Revenue from new business
Fulfillment	Client satisfaction rating (NPS)	Client referrals or retention
Financial Health	Invoiced vs. collected cash	Monthly profit or burn rate
Team	Team check-ins completed	Turnover or employee reviews

Lead indicators are what you can influence directly.
Lag indicators are the outcomes that follow.
Track both—but focus on leads. That's where action lives.

Step 3: Keep It Simple

Track three to five numbers that matter. Not thirty-seven that look good.
You don't need a dashboard with eighteen tabs. You need a short list of metrics that tell you whether you're winning—or drifting.

My Favorite Rule:

If you can't make a decision from it, it's not a real KPI.
Good KPIs create clarity. They force choices. They expose where you're stuck.

Weekly Rhythm:

Pick a day.
Block thirty minutes.
Pull the numbers.
Ask: Are we winning? If not, why?

Then fix it. That's the rhythm of ownership.

Reflection Prompt: Numbers

- What are three numbers that actually show whether your business is moving forward or stuck in place?
- Which ones are you looking at too often?
- Which ones are you ignoring?

Once you're tracking the right metrics, start with the one that reveals whether your growth is sustainable or just expensive.

Track This First: CAC to LTV

Marketing isn't about looking good.

It's about math.

If you don't know what it costs to acquire a customer—and what that customer is worth over time—you're not building a business. You're gambling.

This is where the **CAC to LTV** ratio comes in.

What It Means

- **CAC (Customer Acquisition Cost):** What you spend to acquire one customer
- **LTV (Lifetime Value):** What that customer is worth over the life of their relationship with your business

The ratio tells you how many dollars you get back for every dollar you spend.

The Basic Formula

CAC to LTV Ratio = LTV ÷ CAC

What a Healthy Ratio Looks Like

RATIO	MEANING
1:1	Breaking even. Not scalable.
1:2	Weak. One mistake from a loss.
1:3	Strong. This is the healthy benchmark.
1:4+	Scalable. Time to invest with confidence.

Example:

You spent $20,000 on marketing and signed ten clients:

CAC = 20,000 ÷ 10 = $2,000

Each client is worth $6,000 in net revenue:

LTV = $6,000

Ratio = 6,000 ÷ 2,000 = 3:1

That's a strong signal. You can scale with confidence.

Industry Context Matters

- In **personal injury**, referral fees are part of CAC, even if you didn't pay for ads.
- In **med spas**, referral fees aren't allowed. Your CAC comes from:
- Paid ads
- Content and organic traffic
- Events or outreach
- Staff time and commissions

That's why **retention and upsells** matter so much more in medical—because your margin is built over time, not all at once.

What Most People Miss

LTV doesn't stop at the first transaction.
It includes:

- Repeat business

- Upsells and cross-sells
- Referrals

If one in four clients sends you another, your LTV is higher than you think.

Your best clients are your unpaid marketing team. Treat them like it.

In my businesses, CAC doesn't vary much by lead source, but it does vary by **referral partner**. Some consistently send aligned, profitable clients. Others send volume that costs more than it's worth.

Sometimes, refining your **referral ecosystem** boosts your margin more than tweaking your ad campaign.

Expanded Formula for Smart Builders

True LTV = Net Revenue + Repeat Business + (Referral Rate × Referral Value)

Why You Should Track This

- It tells you what it really costs to grow
- It helps you spend with confidence—or pull back with clarity
- It gives you a simple, scalable benchmark to review every month

If you're not tracking CAC to LTV, you're scaling blind.

Reflection Prompt: Assessing Your Starting Point

- What's your total marketing + sales spend this month?
- How many new clients did you sign?
- What's your CAC—and how does it compare to your average revenue per client?

- Which referral partners or lead sources deliver your best clients?

I faced new challenges—building systems, managing a team, and creating sustainable growth. What kept me moving forward was a commitment to reinvesting in myself. Attending conferences, hiring coaches, and reading about leadership gave me the tools to pivot when necessary and avoid stagnation. For example, joining a mastermind group provided insights I couldn't have gained alone, helping me scale my business while staying grounded in my values.

How to Transition to Business Ownership:

1. **Delegate and Trust Your Team:** Identify tasks that don't require your unique skills and delegate them.
2. **Build Systems and Processes:** Create workflows that allow the business to function independently of you.
3. **Step Back to Scale:** Focus on strategic growth and long-term goals rather than daily operations.

Positioning People in Their Zone of Genius

Every person on your team has unique strengths and talents—their *zone of genius*. This is the space where they perform at their highest level, where their skills and passions align to create maximum impact. As a leader, not only is it your responsibility to find your zone of genius, but your ability to recognize and nurture these zones in others can transform your business.

When people operate within their zone of genius, they're not just more productive—they're more engaged, creative, and fulfilled. On the other hand, assigning people to tasks that don't align with their strengths often leads to frustration, burnout, and mediocre results. It's a lose-lose for both the individual and the organization.

The best leaders know how to uncover these unique abilities and position their team members in roles where they can thrive. This isn't just about getting work done; it's about creating an environment where every team member feels valued and energized by the contributions they're making.

Practical Steps to Uncover and Leverage the Zone of Genius

1. **Have Open Conversations**
   - Sit down with your team members and ask them reflective questions:
   - *"What tasks make you feel energized and excited?"*
   - *"Which parts of your role do you enjoy the most?"*
   - *"Are there areas where you feel you're underutilizing your strengths?"*
   - These conversations often reveal hidden talents and passions that aren't obvious in day-to-day work.

2. **Observe Natural Strengths**
   - Pay attention to where your team members excel without much effort.
   - Look for patterns: Who consistently delivers outstanding results? Who steps up when certain challenges arise?

3. **Align Roles with Strengths**
   - Restructure responsibilities so team members spend more time in their zone of genius.
   - Delegate tasks outside their strengths to others who excel in those areas.

4. **Invest in Development**
   - Provide training, mentorship, or resources to help team members deepen their expertise in their genius zones.
   - Encourage continuous growth and learning to refine their skills.

5. **Create a Collaborative Environment**
   - Recognize that no one can be great at everything. Encourage team members to rely on each other's strengths to fill gaps and create synergy.

Unlocking Potential

Early in my leadership journey, I encountered a paralegal on my team who struggled with administrative tasks. Initially, I saw this as a performance issue. Frustrated, I considered transitioning her out of the team. But instead of acting immediately, I decided to have a conversation.

Through that conversation, I discovered her passion for client communication. She thrived in situations where she could engage directly with people, offering support and clarity. Recognizing this, I adjusted her role to focus on intake and client care. The transformation was remarkable.

Within weeks, she became one of the team's most valuable members. She not only excelled in her new role but also inspired her colleagues with her enthusiasm. Her confidence grew, and she found joy in her work—a direct result of operating in her zone of genius.

This experience taught me the importance of taking the time to uncover individual strengths and aligning roles with those strengths. It's a practice I've carried forward ever since.

The Ripple Effect of Genius

When you position people in their zone of genius, the benefits extend far beyond individual performance:

- **Increased Engagement**: Team members feel more connected to their work, which boosts morale and retention.
- **Enhanced Collaboration**: People working in their genius zones are more likely to support and complement each other's strengths.
- **Improved Results**: Aligning tasks with strengths leads to greater efficiency and better outcomes.

A culture that prioritizes alignment between roles and talents creates an environment where excellence becomes the standard for everyone involved

Preparing for the Next Jump

Every stage of growth brings new opportunities—and new risks. Scaling isn't the end of the journey; it's a launchpad for what's next. Staying open to the unknown and embracing new challenges ensures your business and personal growth remain intertwined.

After scaling my business through my JUMP Method, I found myself drawn to new ventures, including partnerships and investments. One opportunity seemed out of reach—a joint venture with a nationally recognized brand. I almost walked away, doubting whether I was ready. But I remembered the mindset shifts I had practiced and leaned into the discomfort. Following my JUMP Method in relation to this new venture, that partnership became one of the most transformative experiences of my career, opening doors I never imagined. My zone of genius is in scaling law firms, but I realized that it also extends to any business that has been successful for at least a year, looking to scale. The JUMP Method and my values resonate with all entrepreneurs looking to not only scale their businesses but also to scale their lives for the better.

Entrepreneurship is not just about building a business; it's about building a life and legacy that reflect your values. Scaling your business is an opportunity to deepen your impact, inspire others, and create a culture that thrives long after you're gone.

The Staircase: Harvest, Pause, or Pivot

Growth can be intoxicating. The same drive that pulled me out of familiarity can, if I'm not careful, keep me sprinting long after I've arrived. Just like people can be addicted to their suffering, entrepreneurs can get addicted to their growth—the chase, the build, the next mountain.

Real growth isn't always acceleration; sometimes it's alignment. Sometimes it looks like slowing down to see further. Sometimes it's partnering so the vision multiplies. And sometimes—depending on the season—it's harvesting what you've built. Growth isn't a straight line up; it's a staircase. Each step asks a different version of you to lead: one that knows when to climb and when to build.

I don't know exactly what the next season will look like when this book lands in your hands. Maybe deeper partnerships that mirror my vision. Maybe freeing up capital to build other ventures. Maybe staying the course with more clarity and peace. What I do know is this: I built an eight-figure firm fast, and the jump didn't end there. The next leap might be louder—or quieter. Either way, it's still a leap.

Because the jump was never just about going faster. It was about evolving on purpose.

The JUMP Takeaway

You don't need permission.

Build the list. Feed the fire. Burn clean.

The real transformation comes when you shift from trying to prove others wrong to realizing that it was never about them in the first place. Your triggers often stem from something unhealed or missing inside of you. That lack isn't a flaw; it's an invitation to grow.

It doesn't matter what your story is—you were born to figure it out. You choose how you allow your story to define you. You can let it cage you in self-pity, or you can mine it for the raw materials that will build your strength.

You don't need more external validation. You need to build your mental resume, a record of every time you did something hard, figured it out, and kept going. Once you start to see your own power clearly, you'll realize you can do anything you put your mind to and understand that your triggers often stem from something missing inside of you. That lack isn't a flaw—it's an invitation. Then, ask yourself three powerful questions:

1. *What's my next jump?*
2. *How will I use the lessons from this journey to tackle the next challenge?*
3. *What legacy do I want to leave behind for my team, my family, and the world?*

It's time to take the JUMP and remember these ten unshakeable truths:

1. **Your story isn't your excuse—it's your edge.**
   Everything you've lived through was training for the leap.
2. **You don't need permission to leave the box—you need courage.**
   Waiting for validation is how dreams die.

3. **A leap without preparation is just a fall.**
    Plan like your life depends on it—because the one you
    want does.
4. **Fear is a signal, not a stop sign.**
    The scarier it feels, the closer you are to something
    meaningful.
5. **You can't think your way into a new life—you have
    to act your way there.**
    Small, consistent leaps create big transformations.
6. **The safety net is a cage when it stops you from
    growing.**
    Comfort is addictive—but it's not the same as
    fulfillment.
7. **Your why is your anchor.**
    When everything feels shaky, purpose is what holds
    you steady.
8. **Mindset isn't positive thinking—it's ownership.**
    The shift happens when you stop blaming and start
    building.
9. **You are not behind. You are just waiting to begin.**
    Start from where you are. Start now.
10. **You deserve to jump simply because you exist.**
    You don't have to earn a better life. You just have to
    claim it.

You're ready! It's time to take the JUMP, and if you are looking
for expert guidance on taking the first step, let me assist you on
your journey.

The JUMP never ends—you just keep landing higher.

Remember the sticky note?

I threw it away.

Not out of anger—out of clarity.

That sticky note used to haunt me. Its silence. Its smallness. The way it reduced everything I had built to a few scribbled names.

No plan. No vision. No acknowledgment.

Now it fuels me.

It reminds me that no one else gets to define my worth—or write my future.

It didn't end me.

It freed me.

It didn't define me.

It revealed me.

It didn't hold me back.

It helped me leap.

That note wasn't a betrayal. It was a mirror.

It showed me the difference between **belonging** and **staying too long**.

This book began with **the Signal**—that quiet ache that says: *You're made for more.*

It pulled you out of autopilot.

It broke through the **Gravity of Familiarity**.

It cracked the shell of everything safe but misaligned.

If you're still thinking about it—that was your Signal.

You don't need a perfect plan.

You don't need permission.

You need honesty. Courage. Commitment.

And then—just one move.

You're not falling.

You're jumping.

And that's the difference.

Falling is accidental.

Jumping is chosen.

Your jump won't look like mine.

It shouldn't.

But if it **scares you and calls you forward at the same time**, you're right on time—and remember to pack your parachute.

Pack Your Parachute: Will the Business Hold When You Let Go?

Before you jump, there's one thing you'd better make sure of:

Did you pack your parachute?

Because here's the truth most entrepreneurs avoid:

You don't go splat because you weren't brave enough.

You go splat because you weren't ready.

You didn't build systems.

You didn't delegate effectively.

You didn't prepare your team to fly without you.

You jumped, hoping it would all work out.

And hope's not a parachute.

The Parachute Test

Here's the drill I now run in my businesses—law firm, med spa, or anything I build:

"If I had to disappear for thirty days, starting tomorrow, what would fall apart?"

Not what would slow down—what would break?

This is your parachute test. It's how you check if you're building a business that can actually support your leap.

Your Pre-Jump Checklist

Ask yourself honestly:

- Leadership: *Who takes the wheel if I step away? Do they know our mission? Are they empowered to decide without me?*
- Marketing: *Are leads still coming in? Is our strategy system-ized, or am I the campaign?*
- Cash Flow: *Are we forecasting? Do we know our runway? Who's watching AR and burn rate?*
- Client Experience: *Are we delivering consistent service, or does client trust vanish without my name attached?*

- Daily Ops: *Do people know what to do without asking me? Are there processes or just habits that we hope hold?*

If you have to micromanage, approve every dollar, or solve every crisis, your parachute's still full of holes.

What Happened When I Didn't Pack Mine

I once delegated too early, thinking I had my systems in place. We were growing fast. I stepped out of casework to build the firm. It felt like the right move … until we couldn't afford the overhead. I had to jump back in.

It wasn't a failure—it was a lesson.

Delegation without financial margin isn't leadership; it's wishful thinking.

That moment taught me:

The jump has to be backed by a system strong enough to catch you.

You're Not Just Jumping—You're Building Mid-Air

Entrepreneurship isn't a leap with a soft landing.

It's a free fall with a backpack full of parts.

You assemble it as you go.

You delegate mid-air.

You install the altimeter.

You pray the wings hold.

But if you've packed it right—if the rhythms, numbers, roles, and trust are in place—you don't just survive the jump.

You start to fly.

The Bold Jump, the Quiet Preparation

The leap gets the spotlight.

The packing gets overlooked.

But here's what I know now:
The preparation is what makes the leap worth it.
It's not sexy.
It's not loud.
It doesn't get likes.
But it's everything.
Because when you've packed the parachute right—
you don't have to hope you'll make it.
You know.

The Quiet Room: The Loneliness of an Entrepreneur

No one tells you how loud the silence gets after you make the jump.
You walk out of the nine-to-five with fire in your chest.
You're finally free. You're building something that's yours.
And then … you look around.
There's no team yet.
There's no roadmap.
There's just you. And the weight of every decision.
Who do I hire?
Am I charging enough?
Should I push forward or pull back?
Am I doing this right?
Am I crazy?
It's not just lonely—it's vulnerable.
Because the higher you go, the fewer people there are who really understand what you're carrying.

Even Surrounded, You Can Still Feel Alone

What surprised me most wasn't the early loneliness; it was the loneliness in the middle.

Once the business grew, I had a team. I had meetings. I had momentum.
But I didn't have peers.
I didn't have people to whom I could say,

"I'm scared."
"I feel like I'm faking it."
"I'm not sure this is working."
Everyone looked to me for answers.
But no one was looking out for mine.
And during one of the hardest parts of the climb, I fell back into an old pattern:
I isolated.
Not just from friends or community …
At times, even from my own family.
I'd come home, physically present but mentally spinning—stuck in my head, replaying decisions, obsessing over outcomes.
My wife could feel it. My kids sensed the distance.
And I told myself the lie so many entrepreneurs believe:

"I'm doing this for them."
But the truth was—I was disappearing.
From the people I love. From myself.

The Trap of Isolating … Together

What made it harder to spot this time was that I wasn't alone—I had partners.
We were in the trenches, building side by side.
We talked every day. We solved problems. We moved fast.
But emotionally? We were still isolating—together.
Sometimes, when you have partners, you build a bunker.
You keep the stress inside. You carry it between you.
You think you're protecting the team by holding it all together,

but really, you're cutting off connection from the outside world and each other.

And over time, that pressure builds. That bubble gets heavy.

I realized we didn't just need connection outside the partnership—we needed radical honesty inside it, too.

And Then I Remembered: I've Been Here Before

This wasn't new.

This was an old pattern—one I thought I had left behind.

But pressure has a way of pulling you back into familiar shadows.

And that's when I knew it was time to return to the work.

I stepped back into the breath.

Back into my mindset practice.

Back into the mirror.

Not because I was broken—but because I was building again.

And the version of me I needed for this next chapter wasn't the one who could carry everything; it was the one who knew when to let others in.

You're Not Weak—You're Awake

Loneliness doesn't mean you're failing.

It means you care deeply.

It means you're carrying something heavy.

It means you're walking a road not many people choose.

But just because it's rare doesn't mean you have to walk it alone.

You can be ambitious and still present.

You can lead powerfully and still be vulnerable.

You can build with drive—without losing your connection.

Operating Rhythms: How to Scale Without Chaos

If you feel like you're building the plane while flying it, welcome to entrepreneurship.

There comes a point in every growing business where nothing feels stable. You're chasing fires, everyone's "busy," and there's no clear alignment. Goals might be vivid in your head, but your team isn't sure what winning looks like. That's not a people problem—it's a rhythm problem.

The Wake-Up Call: Learning the Value of Structured Meetings

Before we merged, I couldn't even recall the last time I held a proper meeting. I thought meetings were interruptions, time wasted instead of spent on real work. Then my partner taught me a simple truth:

Structured meetings are the heartbeat of a growing business.

They aren't about wasting time; they create a shared cadence, align priorities, and build accountability. In fact, when I implemented the same Entrepenurial Operating System EOS system my partner had been using prior to our merger at my med spa, my revenue increased by 25 percent. We plugged critical holes in our processes that had been bleeding cash and opportunity.

That lesson reshaped my thinking. With the right operating rhythm, you stop managing chaos and start driving momentum.

Our Multi-Tiered Meeting Structure

We built a meeting system that keeps our firm aligned and accountable. We run EOS-style leadership meetings at both the law firm and the med spa. Even though the med spa has fewer employees, the principles of alignment, accountability, and transparency remain essential. In addition, each pod at the law firm meets weekly to ensure that even the smallest teams are on track.

1. Weekly Leadership Meeting (EOS Style) – Law Firm

- Who: The core leadership team at the law firm
- When: Every Monday
- Focus: Reviewing the scorecard, KPIs, and key operational metrics; discussing strategic issues; setting quarterly "rocks" and aligning on immediate priorities.
- Why it matters: This meeting forces us to face reality with data, make informed decisions, and ensure that our vision is executed at the highest level.

2. Weekly Leadership Meeting (EOS Style) – Med Spa

- Who: The leadership or management team at the med spa
- When: Once a week, on a consistent day
- Focus: Even with a smaller team, this meeting centers on reviewing key metrics, operational updates, and addressing immediate challenges. It ensures that every team member understands their role and that the business remains agile and aligned.
- Why it matters: Structured meetings at the med spa create clarity and accountability—key factors that contributed to our 25 percent revenue boost.

3. Biweekly Team Meeting (Level 10 with Attorneys) – Law Firm

- Who: Our attorneys and core operational team
- When: Every other week
- Focus: Using the Level 10 meeting format to review wins,

discuss challenges, and align on project progress; quickly resolving obstacles and clarifying next steps.

- Why it matters: This format creates transparency across the team, ensures accountability, and helps maintain momentum without overloading everyone with meetings.

4. Weekly Pod Meetings – Law Firm

- Who: Each smaller "pod" or subgroup within the law firm
- When: Once a week
- Focus: Localized discussions that focus on immediate tasks, client updates, and specific challenges unique to each pod.
- Why it matters: These meetings ensure that every level of the organization—down to the most granular team—remains aligned and accountable. They're the pulse check that keeps the entire firm functioning as one cohesive unit.

Too Many Meetings: Finding the Right Balance

While structured meetings are essential, there's a fine line between establishing a productive rhythm and overloading your team with meetings.

One common pitfall is the tendency to fill meeting time with unnecessary chatter or status updates that add little value. When meetings drag on, participants often feel obligated to "fill the silence," even when the agenda is already covered. This not only wastes time but also dilutes the focus of the meeting. To combat this:

- Keep It Purposeful: Every meeting should have a clear agenda and outcome. If a topic isn't actionable, save it for another forum.

- Timebox Discussions: Stick strictly to your schedule. Overrun sessions are often filled with filler rather than solutions.
- Encourage Conciseness: Train your team to get to the point and focus on key issues that drive results.

Ensure that every meeting is laser-focused and drives real momentum.

The Mindset Shift: Structure Creates Freedom

I used to resist more meetings, believing they stole time from what I loved doing. But my partner's lesson reshaped my thinking:

Structure isn't a prison; it's a performance tool.

When your operating rhythm is locked in:

- Everyone knows exactly what they should be doing.
- You stop firefighting and start predicting problems before they become emergencies.
- Accountability becomes a natural part of the culture.
- Most importantly, you free up mental space for strategic thinking.

Start Simple. Stay Consistent.

If you're not ready to implement a full-scale system immediately, begin small:

- Start with a weekly leadership meeting (EOS style).
- Use a shared to-do tracker (Ninety.io, ClickUp, Asana—whichever fits your style) to ensure every goal and number has clear ownership.

Meetings without ownership create noise; meetings with rhythm create momentum.

Rhythm Is What Makes Growth Sustainable

Many businesses can hustle their way to $1M. But to scale beyond that—and not lose your mind—you need a consistent operating rhythm.

You need a way to pulse with your team, track progress, and keep the vision front and center.

Chaos can drive short-term growth, but a well-established rhythm is what builds a business that lasts.

Leveraging Dashboards for Accountability and Growth

One of the most powerful tools we use to keep our business on track is our Power BI dashboard. It's not just a tool for daily tracking; it's a suite of tailored dashboards that drive accountability across every area of our operation and are central to our quarterly strategy meetings.

After business coaching with Mike Morse and Fireproof Mastermind, we began tracking a specific set of KPIs that transformed our approach. These metrics have become the backbone of our data-driven decision-making and include:

- Marketing KPIs: ROI, cost-per-lead, conversion rates, and campaign effectiveness.
- Pod Performance KPIs: Profitability per pod, attorney performance, client satisfaction, and revenue per case.
- Intake KPIs: Call response times, conversion rates from inquiry to client, and overall efficiency in capturing new business.
- Referral Source KPIs: Quality and volume of referrals, and alignment with our core values and long-term strategy.

These KPIs are not static figures; they are regularly reviewed at our quarterly meetings to plug process gaps, refine strategies, and ensure that every department is aligned with our overall vision.

At our quarterly meetings, we dive deep into these dashboards, identifying trends, plugging operational holes, and adjusting our tactics for continuous improvement. This routine has been a key driver in our success.

Making these dashboards accessible to every team—from marketing to intake to our pods—means we foster a culture of transparency and accountability. Everyone knows the numbers that matter, and that shared visibility turns instinct into actionable insights.

Final Thought: You Can Jump Without Disappearing

Entrepreneurship will test your strength, your belief, your endurance—and your heart.

But you don't have to disappear to prove how strong you are.

You don't have to isolate, even in partnership, to protect what you're building.

You can lead with clarity.

You can build with intention.

You can stay open, even when it's hard.

Because the goal was never just to jump.

It was to land as yourself—and bring others with you.

This isn't the end.

This is the next door.

This is your **Infinite Growth Cycle**.

You answered the Signal.

You made the Jump.

Now build what only you can build.

You're ready to JUMP.

You've faced your fears, rewritten your story, and unlocked your Zone of Genius.

But the journey doesn't end here—it begins now.

Join the movement at *www.jumpwithblake.com*—get exclusive resources, live coaching, and the support of others making their leap.

Subscribe on YouTube (@jumpwithblake.com) for weekly tools, mindset shifts, and real stories of transformation.

This isn't just a book. It's a launchpad.

Let's build the life you were meant for—together.

AFTERWORD: THE WAY BACK TO MYSELF

Every leap we take—into business, into leadership, into growth—pulls us forward.

But what I've learned is that without moments of deep stillness, we can lose the very part of ourselves we jumped for.

This final reflection is about that stillness. About what I found when I stopped building and started listening.

I didn't go into the jungle before the leap.

I went **as I was building**—

when growth was real,

the team was expanding,

and everyone was counting on me.

Because even in success, I was slipping.

I had jumped.

But somewhere inside the jump, I began to disappear.

Not all at once—

but slowly, beneath the weight of proving, producing, pushing.

So, I walked away.

No podcast. No planner.

Just a hammock. A notebook. Filtered water that tasted like metal.

Silence so loud it shook me.

And then—

me.

Not the performer. Not the builder.

Just the observer.

Watching thoughts pass like clouds.

Listening to lies that I once called truth.

I'd learned how to scale a business.

But I had never learned to sit.
Turns out, the leap wasn't the hardest part.
Staying whole inside it was.
If you're building right now—
growing, leading, leaping—
don't forget:
Stillness isn't weakness.
It's where your truth lives.
And the most important part of the jump
is remembering how to come home.
To you.

Branded Principles Map + JUMP Method Framework

The JUMP Method: A Framework for Reinvention

Phase	Concept	Definition	Core Question
J	Justify Your Why	Define the deep reason you need to leap.	Why can't I stay where I am?
U	Uncover Limiting Beliefs	Identify internal scripts that keep you stuck.	What story am I living that no longer serves me?
M	Mindset Shift	Shift from victim to creator. Reclaim your power.	Am I reacting, or am I creating?
P	Plan + Take Small Leaps	Build the systems and confidence to act intentionally.	What's the smallest bold move I can take now?

Core Metaphors, Mindsets, and Identity Shifts

CONCEPT	DEFINITION	SIGNATURE LINE	ECHO/PULL QUOTE	APPEARS
The Fog	The limbo-like state before you leap.	The Fog doesn't mean you're lost ...		Chapter One
The Signal	The quiet ache that something must change.	The moment you heard the Signal ...	You don't need the plan. You just need to listen.	Chapter One

CONCEPT	DEFINITION	SIGNATURE LINE	ECHO/PULL QUOTE	APPEARS
The False Finish Line	Success on paper, emptiness inside.	This was my False Finish Line.	Success without alignment is just burnout in disguise.	Chapter Three
The Gravity of Familiarity	The emotional pull to stay where it's safe.	That was just the Gravity of Familiarity …	Comfort is the gravity that kills change.	Chapter Four, Nine
High Performer's Armor	Using output to prove worth.	My high performance had become my armor.	Productivity without purpose is just armor dressed up as progress.	Chapter Four, Seven
Internal Scripts	Limiting beliefs absorbed unconsciously.	You're not broken. You're just living by an outdated internal script.		Chapter Six
Growth Trial	Failure redefined as iterative growth.	Every setback is a growth trial.	Growth is just feedback with sharp edges.	Chapter Thirteen
Clarity Threshold	The moment you can no longer pretend.	The Clarity Threshold hits you in the gut.		Chapter Nine

CONCEPT	DEFINITION	SIGNATURE LINE	ECHO/PULL QUOTE	APPEARS
The Commitment Contract	A vow to stop waiting.	Silent but irreversible.	I had already signed the Contract.	Chapter Ten, Thirteen
Burn and Build Principle	Burn the fallback. Build what's next.	I had to burn the safety plan.	Jumping doesn't mean chaos. It means Burn and Build.	Chapter Nine, Eleven
I'm the F***ing Bat	The shift from reaction to precision.	I strike with intention.	Precision replaces chaos. That's the shift.	Chapter Seven
The Ownership Shift	Operator / Visionary leader.	This wasn't delegation—it was the Ownership Shift.	Letting go of control isn't weak-ness—it's wisdom.	Chapter Twelve

ACKNOWLEDGMENTS

To my daughter, Charley—you are such an incredible person. Your curiosity in life reminds me to stay curious every day. You are a constant reminder to enjoy the journey, not just the destination.

To my daughter, Noah—your birth came during the rebirth of my own life. I can't wait to share this journey with you and watch the beautiful bond you have with your sister continue to grow.

To my wife—I have no idea how you dealt with me during the most difficult parts of this journey. But your commitment to your own healing is what opened the door for mine. You are truly the yin to my yang and the grounding force that allows me to continue jumping.

To my father—you were my best friend, and you will live in my heart forever. I inherited my love of people from you. In your pain and suffering, you reminded me of what I'm living for. In your passing, you breathed life into my dreams. I am forever grateful to have had such an amazing father.

To my mom—thank you for supporting me, even when the things I reach for feel uncertain or even frightening. I know your fear has always come from a place of unconditional love. Right after completing this book, I called you about a big decision I was trying to make, and your response was, "I trust you." Those words gave me chills. They showed me that the transformation I've gone through has invited you to grow alongside me—not because you ever lacked as a mother but because you've continued to evolve in how you love, support, and believe in me. I keep growing every day, and it's beautiful to witness how your love keeps growing too.

To my business partners—thank you for pushing me to be better every single day. Entrepreneurship is the greatest mirror, reflecting not only our strengths but also the places we need to grow. It is an honor to continue this journey alongside you and to keep growing together.

To my siblings—you have become such a strong support network, and I'm so grateful to have you in my life. I've watched you face life's greatest struggles with courage and resilience, and I'm inspired by the way you continue to move forward in faith. Though we are separated by geography and busy with our families, I feel closer to you now than ever before. Keep pushing, keep leaning into faith, and know that I am excited to watch you grow, evolve, and live lives fully aligned with who you are. Love you all so much.

To my mentors at Fireproof and to Steven Hurwitz—thank you for showing me how to lead with purpose and systems, and for helping me think beyond the day-to-day.

To my best friends, Brian Cahill and Stuart Dyer—you both have a unique gift of being master connectors, and so many of the most meaningful relationships in my life were born from your friendships. You've seen me at my worst and my best, and you've always been there. Forever brothers.

To Mary Holyrod and Jana Wilson. Thank you for walking beside me through the emotional valleys of this journey. You helped me not only navigate the hardest moments but also see the beauty in the struggle. This book would not exist without the light you shared with me. I also hold deep gratitude for the countless others who offered encouragement, perspective, and love when I needed it most. Your voices echo through these pages.

To Alex Myrin — brother for life, my friend. Your courage to face the darkest parts of yourself inspired me to do the same. Your strength, honesty, and unwavering heart will always be a light I carry with me.

To my team—thank you for believing in this vision when it was messy, uncertain, and new. You've helped build something real, and I'm proud of the culture we've created together.

To my mentors—both those I've met and those I've read—your insight and examples helped shape this book and the mindset behind it.

And to the reader—thank you for having the courage to jump. I hope this book serves as a mirror, a guide, and a spark on your journey

# ABOUT THE AUTHOR

I was born and raised on the Connecticut shoreline, the youngest of three biological siblings in a large, hardworking family. My dad was the kind of man who worked all day, then came home and mowed the lawn in his suit. A fireman, police officer, and later the owner of a funeral home, his unwavering work ethic instilled in me lessons that shaped my own drive. My mom, who worked for a doctor, came from a big family and carried a quiet strength of her own.

Growing up, my parents let me figure out life the old-fashioned way. I taught myself sports by trial and error. I learned how to learn by failing, again and again. There was no pressure to perform in school, no expectation to strive for excellence. No one helped me with homework or taught me how to ride a bike. For much of my life, I saw that as a disadvantage. But in hindsight, it was one of my greatest gifts.

That self-reliance, that ability to embrace failure as a teacher, became the foundation for my success as an entrepreneur. When it came time to break free from my nine-to-five and step into the life I had always envisioned, I realized I had already been training for it my entire life.

My view of life has transformed from that of a victim, dictated by circumstances, to that of a person empowered by his choices. I wake up every day with childlike curiosity about what I am going to build and create, living in alignment with a clearly defined why.

I am extremely self-driven and have taught myself how to live a disciplined yet authentic life. My mission is to protect those who feel victimized by their circumstances and empower them to stand up to their fears, stepping into the life they dream of. I do this as a lawyer, a business coach, and an entrepreneur.

I have built multiple six- and seven-figure businesses, and my law practice will well eclipse the eight-figure mark this year. I have grown my firm from just three people to almost eighty in three years and have recovered over $100 million for people who have been taken advantage of by insurance companies, helping them reclaim not just what they have lost but also their sense of power.

But none of it would mean anything without my family. I have a beautiful wife who grounds me, truly the yin to my yang. And my daughters? They are my greatest gift and my biggest teachers. They remind me every day why I push forward, why I grow, and why I will never stop building.

My mom and dad have always been my greatest cheerleaders. I am sure I scared them as I pushed the boundaries of what they were comfortable with, but they were always the first to support me as I broke through perceived barriers. My dad, who recently passed, taught me resilience through his actions, and my mom continues to inspire me with her unwavering strength.

I honor them both by continuing to push forward.

Beyond my law firm, I own a med spa and chiropractic office in partnership with a woman who has shattered every perceived barrier, a woman of color, a stage 4 cancer survivor, and a living testament to resilience and strength. My law partner is another example of what it means to live a life of authenticity and purpose, a man who looked at himself in the mirror a few years ago and had the courage to change everything. He is proof that we can build a life rather than just live one.

I surround myself with people who inspire me, and discomfort is my greatest addiction. I have lived in solitude for a week to test my ability to disconnect, and I just completed a marathon. I embrace discomfort because in it, I find growth.

I don't believe in failure because I don't ever quit. I live life with a hypothesis mindset; every challenge is just data, every setback, part of the process. In fact, I don't even believe in barriers. They are just signs, teaching me to shift and grow.

Everything I have built, every leap I have taken, has been grounded in one simple truth: The only way to change your life is to JUMP!

ENDNOTES

1   Haimovitz, K., & Dweck, C. S. (2016). "Parents' views of failure predict children's fixed intelligence mindsets and negative feelings about failure." Journal of Child and Family Studies, 25(9), 2774–2787. *https://doi.org/10.1007/s10826-016-0513-7*

2   "The Legacy of Trauma: Emerging Research." Monitor on Psychology. American Psychological Association, 2011 *https://www.apa.org/monitor/2019/02/legacy-trauma*

3   Zedelius, C. M., Veling, H., & Aronson, J. (2025). "How rethinking difficulties can shape important life outcomes." Trends in Cognitive Sciences. *https://www.cell.com/trends/cognitive-sciences/fulltext/S1364-6613%2825%2900145-7*

4   Barker, R. C. (2004). *The Power of Decision.* New York, NY. TarcherPerigee. (Original work published 1968.)

5   Greg Crabtree, *Simple Numbers, Straight Talk, Big Profits.* Greenleaf Book Group Press, 2011.

6   Doug Tatum, *No Man's Land: Where Growing Companies Fail* (Portfolio, 2007).

7   Startup Genome. *Startup Genome Report Extra on Premature Scaling* (2011).

9 798999 052018